Special Occasion Cookbook

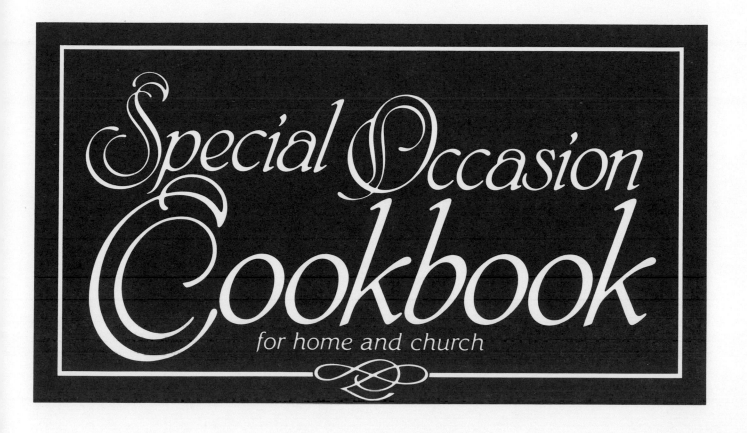

Special Occasion Cookbook

for home and church

Richard Brown
and
Melva Cook

BROADMAN PRESS
Nashville, Tennessee

Dedicated to
Anne Sneed Brown
mother of Richard
and
to the memory of
Irene Frazier Cook
mother of Melva

© Copyright 1983 • Broadman Press
All rights reserved
4270-01
ISBN: 0-8054-7001-8

Dewey Decimal Classification: 641.5
Subject Headings: COOKERY | | ENTERTAINING
Library of Congress Catalog Card Number: 82-73491
Printed in the United States of America

Cover photograph by Doug Brachey

Contents

Special Occasions
in the Church

Special. Although it has many meanings today, we are using it in the sense that Webster defines it: *Distinguished by some unusual quality, especially in some way superior, being other than the usual.* Special occasions for the church or Christian home are those which are not a part of the regular routine. They are the distinctively different, the superior occasions.

Feasts are an important part of Judeo-Christian history and tradition. The Mosaic law called for three feasts (the Passover; the feast of harvest, later called Pentecost; and the Feast of Tabernacles), and others were added during the Old Testament period. Early Christians seem to have gathered for what became known as the *agape meal.*

In the early history of this country, especially in rural areas, "dinner on the ground" was a common church event. Rural churches seldom had preaching weekly and sometimes less often than once a month, so two or three sermons on Sunday were not unusual when a preacher was available. A morning service, followed by lunch spread under trees on the church lawn, might be followed by two afternoon sermons before the congregation returned home for the evening chores. The annual "protracted" meeting in some areas was a camp meeting with church families camping out for a week or more, eating in family groups or spreading their fare together. It was the social as well as the spiritual highlight of the year.

As churches became more affluent in the twentieth century, dinner on the ground moved inside to new dining rooms, often called fellowship halls. Instead of picnic baskets brought from home, volunteer or part-time hostesses often prepared all or part of church meals in the church kitchen. Covered-dish meals remained popular in some areas, however. Now many large churches have full-time kitchen staff, and meals are served to one group or another, or frequently to many groups, every day.

The life-style of the contemporary family and the expansion of educational activities in the church have brought about the increase in the number of church meals. In most churches, a large percentage of both men and women work outside the home. Committees can meet at noon if a lunch is served; they could not meet at that time otherwise. Evening meetings are more convenient if dinner is served, freeing members to come to the church directly from work. Mother and Daddy could not go home, prepare dinner and feed the children, and get back for an evening meeting. They can pick up the children after school and get to the church for dinner, however. Even in smaller churches which go the covered-dish route, Mother finds preparation of a casserole or dessert much quicker and easier than preparing the entire meal for the family at home.

A by-product of the church meals has been the growth of fellowship. One significant factor in the growth of a church is the spirit of *koinonia*—of love and caring for one another. Such a spirit comes from the Holy Spirit. However, *koinonia* grows as members come to know one another better. Prayer for friends is more meaningful if it is specific, and it becomes specific as we know persons well enough to be aware of their needs. "Bless all who need your help" is worthwhile, but "Bless John and Mary as they face their difficult decision today" is more meaningful to the person praying and contributes to a spirit of oneness. Church meals and other fellowship opportunities provide excellent means of becoming acquainted with persons the church member might not know otherwise. In large churches with age-graded educational activities, members have few contacts with many of their fellow members except at church social occasions.

Entertaining at home is difficult for many families because of limited space and time. Although hospitality is certainly desirable, there are persons who find having friends in (except for one or two at a time) an impossibility. Having a Sunday School class in a home for a class meeting is difficult when houses are small. Church social meetings become even more important in such situations.

Today there are many people who live alone. Many have little opportunity to be with people socially. Church fellowship meals may provide their only opportunity for being a member of a group in a relaxed, informal setting. Such meals also provide opportunities for making friendships which may result in further social occasions.

Our philosophy of church meals and other fellowship occasions involves four *shoulds.*

• Church food for special occasions should be as carefully chosen, as well prepared, and as attractively served as food for any occasion. We do not accept the philosophy that "anything will do" for a church group.

• Special occasions for church groups should be planned and conducted in such a way as to foster fellowship among all members of the group. There may be wide differences in the cultural and socioeconomic backgrounds of members, but each one should be accepted and loved and made to feel comfortable in the group. Care in planning will contribute to a relaxed atmosphere.

• Church food should provide good nutrition. Special occasion meals need not consist of liver and spinach, but they need not consist of too many starches and junk food, or the trite ham and potato salad. With so many Americans needing to lose weight, any church occasion can include options for dieters. Pre-Sunday School fellowship for adults need not be limited to store-bought sweet rolls and doughnuts. Vacation Bible School refreshments and Sunday morning extended session snacks for young children can be more nourishing than artificially flavored sweet drinks and cookies; there are wholesome and appetizing alternatives. Teenagers will eat something other than french fries and colas.

• *Special* need not be expensive. Although *cheap* need not be the sole criteria for selecting food, there is no necessity for disregarding the budget. Careful selection, preparation, and service are more important than cost in making meals special.

Special Occasions in the Christian Home

FOR THE FAMILY

Have you considered the stewardship of your kitchen? of your best dishes, linens, and flatware? Adults certainly have the responsibility for providing nutritious meals for themselves and for children in the home, but good stewardship goes further. Special occasion meals for the family foster family solidarity and oneness. Limiting special meals to times when there are guests says to family members, "Others are more important than we are."

Birthdays; holidays; special achievements in work, school, or civic groups; anniversaries; or sometimes just no occasion at all may be recognized with a special meal. Some families have special dinner at noon every Sunday; others prefer Saturday night. Did you grow up in a chicken-every-Sunday family? Or was it pot roast? Sunday dinner was special in most homes a generation ago.

The menu and table setting for a special family occasion can be anything different from the ordinary. It may be the best china and silver in the dining room or plastic dishes and calico cloth on the patio, but make it as attractive as possible and different from every day.

A family council may be called to plan details. The honoree may be allowed to plan the menu, and all family members may participate in planning table decorations and in preparing the meal. Or some families may prefer to plan details without the knowledge of the honoree, so that everything may be a surprise. Keep his/her likes and dislikes in mind if he/she is not involved in plans. A family policy on the amount of money to be spent may be needed.

Johnny may want a freezer of homemade ice cream to celebrate his Little League team winning the tournament, while Dad may want his favorite roast beef to celebrate his election as director of his church men's group. Mother's vote may be for shrimp creole when her job promotion is being celebrated, while the youngest may want hot dogs to celebrate his entrance to kindergarten. Unless there are allergies or violent dislikes, provide the same meal for everyone on special occasions.

FOR GUESTS

Hospitality was a virtue highly regarded in biblical times. Because of difficulties of travel, Hebrews and early Christians were encouraged to offer hospitality to strangers in their travels. In the early days of our country, pastors and evangelists often stayed in homes of church members when on the church field, living during the week in other communities.

Although needs are different today, there are still opportunities for ministry open to those who are "given to hospitality." Peter's admonition, "Use hospitality to one another without grudging" (1 Pet. 4:9), has not been rescinded.

Jesus' attendance at a wedding feast and at a feast in the home of Matthew, as well as meals in the home of Mary, Martha, and Lazarus; Zacchaeus; and Peter set an example for Christian participation in such occasions.

Christian families have opportunities for special occasions involving persons outside the family circle. In addition to occasions involving members of the extended family or close family friends, there is a need for use of the home as a ministry or outreach approach. Guests may include recently bereaved persons, lonely persons (especially on holidays), newcomers in the church or community, prospective members for the church, Sunday School teachers of family members, persons with whom the family needs to "mend fences," church guests, internationals, single parent families, or any family or individual whom the family would like to know better. If adults in the family are Sunday School teachers, they may be able to have each of their class members as a guest for a meal—individually or in small groups. Guests may be invited for a meal, an open house, dessert, a picnic, or a cookout—any type of entertainment in which the family feels comfortable.

Some families or singles hesitate to entertain because they are limited in space or have no fine furniture, china, linens, or sterling silver. Such factors need not be considered. Use your best without apology. The choicest cut of beef is not necessary for a company meal. Develop a specialty. You'll find your guests will appreciate a delicious stew or casserole. What is better than a kettle of homemade soup and cornbread on a cold night?

Tables can be attractive in the dining room, set with the most expensive crystal and china on fine linen. They can also be attractive on the patio set with colorful homemade placemats or tablecloth and plastic dishes. Study illustrations of table settings in household magazines and use your creativity instead of your credit card. Singles, young married couples, or retired persons may have only a counter in the kitchen, a folding table, or trays; but they will find joy in sharing what they have with guests. Remember, "Better is a dinner of herbs where love is, than a stalled ox and hatred therewith" (Prov. 15:17). Serve one-dish meals or six-course meals, but serve them with love.

Table Decorations

FOR THE CHURCH

Church banquet tables are sometimes the loveliest—and sometimes the tackiest—of all such occasions.

The church food services director may or may not be talented in table decorations, but he/she probably does not have time to decorate elaborately. And sometimes volunteers or easily-conscripted persons suffer from (1) lack of talent, (2) lack of materials, or (3) lack of funds.

Since the cost of table decorations usually must be added to the price of the meal, economy is to be desired. However, who delights in skimpy twines of half-wilted ivy and one candle for every table? Any church can do better!

Most cities and towns have garden clubs, and many churches have members who belong to garden clubs and who have been trained in the art of flower arranging. Find out who these persons are. Enlist them to decorate for your special occasions.

Start a table decoration class, taught by a garden club member. If your church, like many others, depends on senior adults and/or youth to set the tables for all meals, give them some training, but enlist others to participate in training for special occasions at home and at church. Keep a list of persons you'd like to have decorate for your church occasions and enlist them well in advance. Avoid asking the same persons to decorate for every occasion if possible.

If there's an available closet in the church, start collecting everything that might possibly be used. Baskets, vases, flower frogs, bowls, urns, candles, candle holders, and containers of all sizes and shapes may be used.

One church had a most attractive dinner for their fall stewardship banquet. A man from the church membership had collected dozens of small brown glass snuff bottles from a city dump. He used dwarf marigolds and chrysanthemums in them for small arrangements—and they were lovely!

Tin cans may be painted with flat black paint or shiny enamel to make flower containers. Tuna cans work well.

Flowers? Encourage church members to plant an extra bed to share with the church as needed. Promote good stewardship of yards and gardens. Don't forget wild flowers. For a women's luncheon our church used checked tablecloths and wild flowers in abundance. Bare branches may be sprayed white, green, red—whatever colors you're using—and used in vases.

One man who is called on to decorate frequently for his church uses lots of greenery with a few flowers. He buys his greenery from a florist, but most churches will have someone in the membership with greenery to spare. Maybe it's even weeds—just so it isn't ragweed.

Collect objects which can be used as bases for flower arrangements. Two wooden disks about six to eight inches in diameter can be mounted on a twelve-inch dowel to make a spool. Paint them red for Valentine's Day or Fourth of July or Christmas, green or yellow for spring, and orange for fall, using them over and over. Use two or three on each table, with a bowl of greenery and flowers sitting on each.

Have an African violet luncheon—asking members of the church to bring their violets for decorations.

Candles look best when clustered. Instead of three lonely candles scattered down a long table, group them in the center. Use dozens of candles on the head table—all colors and heights. (Freeze them before use and they'll last longer.) Ask church members to bring you their discarded candles. You'll get some you can't use, but you may be able to get a craft class to melt them down and make new ones.

For a Christmas banquet, one volunteer borrowed brass candleholders from many families and used them with red candles on a table at the head of the buffet line. Dozens of candles in brass holders of various heights made a dazzling spectacle. (When borrowing candleholders or other objects, be sure to write the owner's name on a strip of masking tape stuck to the underside.)

Watch the height of arrangements and candles. Don't leave someone hidden behind the fern. Keep arrangements low so that each person can look over them or high on a base of some sort so that guests may see under them.

Consider also the fact that some plants are high allergens. Avoid using Easter lilies, tuberoses, or other plants with strong odors. Many people are allergic to marigolds. You may need to provide a table without flowers for hay fever victims.

China and Silver

One normally associates the following items as basic:
>Punch Bowl, Ladle—Glass or Silver
>Glass Plates
>Glass Cups
>Flatware—Stainless or Silver
>Silver or Glass Serving Trays
>Silver Service
>Ceramic Plates and Cups

True. But do not panic if you don't have any/all of the above. The best way to equip your church kitchen with reception goods is to have a china shower. Why not? Everybody else has them. By beginning in this fashion, everyone may get excited about churchwide receptions.

Contact those interested in contributing financially to this venture. Establish an arrangement with a wholesaler to purchase your necessary goods. You can get a much better deal buying in quantity than each individual person could buy separately. You establish the needed equipment list: eight dozen each of plates, cups, and flatware would be considered an ample starter set. Suggest that each person pay for ½ dozen plates or 2 dozen cups or 1 dozen forks, a punch ladle, or whatever. Several could go in together on the punch bowl or silver trays, nut dish, and spoons. Many times the silver service can be given as a memorial to a church member or Sunday School class.

Don't worry if all items don't balance out on your first shower. Try again; sooner or later you will get it all together.

When purchasing glass plates and cups, buy the *standard* pattern, with the basic slope with no design or pattern. The cups are also basic round and plain. Should you buy a set with a distinctive slant or design, you may pay more initially and upon replacement may not even find it available. By purchasing "everybody's pattern," availability can be easily attained and costs are kept at a lower rate.

Flatware

Institutional stainless flatware can be as nice as silverplated salad forks. The best way to keep the stainless looking nice is to use it solely for church receptions or special occasions. When it starts looking dull and dingy, perk it up with some stainless steel cleaner. Spots and stains will disappear. The original shine will reappear with very little effort on your part.

Silverplated flatware is a most desired option, but securing mixable patterns is the catch. Many members may wish to donate sets of silver, but table presentation is hampered by the look of mismatched patterns. Again, consider the institutional silverplated flatware. It's plain and simple but offers uniformity in design. Should you get enough plates and cups, begin securing sets of stainless or silverplated flatware.

Linens

Have you considered these options for table coverings:
(1) Rental
(2) Church purchase
(3) Church member contribution
Rental works very well for banquets, but all churches need a basic reception tablecloth.

Most churches use two six- or eight-foot tables together as a reception table. Have a cloth made to cover floor to floor or as an overlay on other cloths. This customized look will add an extra dimension of elegance to your table and will also save you from piecemealing and pinning multiple cloths together.

Paper Products

All church receptions vary from the very formal to the most informal. "After Church Fellowship" usually calls for the quick in and out type arrangement of serving. Here is where the basic paper product comes in handy. White Styrofoam, white paper dessert plates, and white plastic ware are considered the basics. You can move next to color/pattern coordinated cup and plate, and plastic plates and clear plastic cups are the extreme. All of these make for easy clean-up and easy availability. For any occasion, select the wares that best suit the occasion: cheap for simple occasions, medium for in-between occasions, and the nicest for those times that are special. *Never* mix styles. You always will cheapen the occasion the high style was intended to be used for.

Setting the Table

Seldom will plates be on the table when guests arrive at a church dinner. More and more churches are using buffet or cafeteria-style service. You will, however, want to have silver, napkins, water or tea glasses or coffee cups, and perhaps salad on the table when guests enter the room. Provide a training session for paid or volunteer helpers who set the tables.

The knife and spoon go to the right of the plate, with the knife blade turned toward the plate. Handles should be about one inch from the edge of the table. Forks belong on the left side of the plate.

If a water or tea glass is used, it should be placed at the tip of the knife. The coffee cup belongs to the right of the spoon and the salad plate at the tip of the fork.

Limited help often requires putting dessert on the table before the meal. Although this arrangement is not as desirable as removal of plates and serving of dessert at the end of the meal, it is permissible. If dessert spoons or forks are available, they may be placed on the dessert plate or, better, horizontal above the plate. If dessert is to be served from the kitchen, forks or spoons will be on the plate.

Napkins go to the left of the fork. If traditionally folded napkins are used, the fold is to be on the side of the fork. However, a variety of styles of folds are possible if cloth napkins are being used.

Getting Ready
to Entertain at Home

This section is written for the person who is new at entertaining at home—the person who is not sure he/she can get it all together. If you're an old hand at party giving, turn the page.

Set a date—Check the family calendar to be sure you have no conflicts. At the last minute you don't want to discover that parents' night at school comes the night you're having guests.

If you're having a guest of honor or others you want to be certain are present, check with them before you definitely set the date.

Issue invitations—You may issue your invitations by mail, telephone, or in person. The cost of postage is making mail invitations less popular; but, if you are a writing-oriented person as opposed to a telephone-oriented person, you may prefer to let the mail carrier do the walking.

Plan menu—Write it down, every item. List recipe source, including page number for each item. Make a shopping list.

Plan table arrangement and decorations. Which tablecloth, napkins, dishes, silver, glassware, etc., will you use? Inspect them. Does the tablecloth need to be laundered or pressed? Does your silver need polishing? What will you use for a centerpiece? If you are buying flowers, order early. If you are depending on flowers from your own yard, what backup plan do you have in case a windstorm or the neighbor's dog gets your tulips the night before your party? (Do you have silk flowers you could use? A variety of candles? A neighbor who would share fresh flowers? Potted African violets in bloom?)

Housecleaning.—What housecleaning do you want done before the party? There's a lot more to it than putting out fresh towels and removing the robes from the bathroom door. Make two lists: *Essentials* and *If-there-is-time.* Doing the windows, waxing kitchen floor, polishing brass doorknobs—you decide what belongs on each list. Then number by priority. Is it more important to you to have the woodwork in the second-floor bedrooms washed or to have the carpet on the stairs shampooed?

List items you need.—Do you need a large cooking pot that you don't have? What about a mixing container for punch? Punch bowl and cups? Coffeemaker? Linens, napkins? Silver trays? Extra silver? Folding tables and chairs for a large sit-down buffet?

In cities and in many smaller towns you will find rental places where anything you need will be available. Or you may live in a community where borrowing from neighbors and friends is taken for granted. Some churches lend or rent such items. List everything you will need and check each off as you arrange to rent or borrow it.

Napkins.—When are paper napkins permissible? For almost any large reception, coffee, or tea, small-size paper napkins of good quality are permissible. If you are using an informal theme, use napkins in bright colors to fit your color scheme. For a more elegant party, use white or pastels, perhaps printed with the name of the honoree and the date. Avoid paper tablecloths for home use.

Try out new dishes.—If you're serving anything that you've never cooked before, try it out. Your family may not like the idea, but don't run the risk of having a problem. (One of us will never forget her humiliation when the recipe that said "serves 16" wasn't quite enough to go around for 12!)

Make a checklist of everything that has to be done.—Include all the housecleaning chores as well as the table arrangements and meal. Now, on at least four sheets of paper, make your countdown list. If the party is on Saturday, make a *Wednesday, Thursday, Friday,* and *Saturday* list. In the order that you need to do them, list all those things that have to be done on your daily sheets. (If you work and are doing your party chores in the evening, you may need to move back to a Monday and Tuesday list. You may even polish silver, wash windows, and iron linens the previous Saturday.)

Enlist help.—If your party is a reception, tea, or even a large buffet meal, you will need kitchen help. For a large party, the hostess needs to be free to greet guests and mingle. The ideal situation is to use a friend who would not normally be included in the party—your cousin Susan who doesn't know the honoree or who isn't in your church, for example. Susan will be ideal if she's given parties herself and knows what needs to be done. She can keep punch cups and silver washed and on the table and keep the punch bowl full, as well as taking care of emergencies that arise. If Susan is calm and fast and efficient, she's a jewel.

If you're having as many as fifty, you probably will need another helper. You may hire a college student or a teenager who is efficient and fast, or you may need a professional maid. If you go either of these routes, make a list of what you want the person to do and go over them with him/her before the party. Or, if you prefer, you may ask three or four of your friends who will be attending the party to take used plates and cups to the kitchen, bring clean ones to the table as needed, and see that food and beverages are replaced.

How many things at the table have to be served? Select one of your friends to serve each. (Some items, such as finger sandwiches, nuts, cookies will be serve-yourself, but you'll want someone to serve coffee, tea, punch, and perhaps cake.) For a buffet, you may want someone to serve a casserole, or you may prefer to have guests serve themselves everything but beverages. Select one of your friends to serve in each spot you need someone. (Don't hesitate; it's considered an honor to be asked to serve.) If your party is to be two or three hours, choose servers for each hour. Select quiet, gracious women (or men) to help.

Keep calm.—Your first big party will likely be a time of stress. Keep as calm as possible. Take time out for your personal prayer and Bible study each day, regardless of how busy you are. Decide what you really want to accomplish on this occasion and pray for God's guidance and blessings. Remember (if you're a female) to allow time to do your hair and nails. Select a dress in which you feel well dressed. You'll be standing a great deal, so be sure your shoes are comfortable. Don't be caught in a standing-up girdle and sitting-down shoes!

Your checklists should give you confidence; but if something goes wrong, learn to laugh about it and go on. The most cherished memories may be the occasion when Mary dropped the pie on the kitchen floor or when the lock on the bathroom broke, leaving Cheryl locked inside.

Have a good time at your party!

Receptions, Teas, Open House

Receptions, teas, open houses. What's the difference? In most communities today, the terms are used interchangeably. Tea may or may not be served at any of them.

Teas are more likely to be held in the afternoon and usually do have hot tea as one choice. Guests are more likely to be women only. An open house is more likely to be in a home, but may be held in a church, especially when the purpose of the party is to give guests an opportunity to see facilities.

AT CHURCH

● Honoring new, departing, or prospective staff members

When a new minister or other staff member arrives on the field, a reception is usually given as a welcome from the church. Members have an opportunity to meet the staff member and his/her family and to express joy in his/her arrival.

Departing staff members are usually honored with a reception, also. Friends want an opportunity to express appreciation for the contribution the staff member has made, not only to the church, but to families and individuals.

Prospective staff members often visit the church and are given a reception to meet the total church membership or, in some instances, the group with whom they would work should they accept the position.

- Honoring new church members or prospective church members

Monthly, quarterly, or annual receptions may be held to recognize new members who have come into the church during that period of time. Some churches also give receptions honoring new persons in the community who have not united with a church. Such receptions promote *koinonia* (fellowship) within the church by helping new persons get acquainted and feel loved and wanted.

- Honoring anniversary of the church or a staff member

The tenth, twenty-fifth, fiftieth, or hundredth anniversaries of the organization of the church are usually celebrated with a reception for the church membership and others in the community. The older the church, the more elaborate the reception usually is.

Anniversaries of pastors or other staff members are often recognized with receptions, also. In addition to church members, staff members holding corresponding positions in other churches may be invited.

- Celebration of completing of building

When a new building is erected or an existing building remodeled or redecorated, the occasion may be celebrated with an open house. Church members and friends may tour the facilities and have an opportunity to greet and express appreciation to the building committee.

- Getting acquainted in new departments and classes

Children's departments usually have an open house soon after Promotion Day so that children may bring their parents to see their new room and meet their teachers. Some churches schedule all such events at the same time and include the entire Sunday School organization. Families may then move together through the building and visit the classroom of every family member. (Prospective members may also be invited.) A time of refreshment and fellowship will follow the tour of rooms.

- Honoring visiting missionary, evangelist, or other church guest

A reception provides an opportunity for all church members, including children, to meet special guests of the church. Such occasions not only make the guest feel welcome and help him/her learn more about the people with whom he/she will be working, but it may lead to individual meaningful contacts.

- Recognizing work of committees, officers

Once a year, some churches provide a reception of persons who have served in leadership roles for the past year. The church can give a well-deserved thank you to volunteer workers.

- Honoring music groups after special services

When choirs give a special concert, the church may say thank you by honoring them at a reception.

- Honoring graduates

Most churches annually honor those who graduate from high school or college. Some churches choose to give a reception in their honor.

- Honoring single adults, senior adults, mothers

Many churches have a day on the calendar to honor each of the above groups. On Sunday afternoon or after the Sunday evening service, a reception may be given to honor those in the special group. Single adults are often recognized the second Sunday in September, senior adults on the first Sunday in May, and mothers on the second Sunday in May.

- Honoring newly married couples in the membership

Because of the importance of young married couples to the church and of the church to young marrieds, a quarterly or annual reception may be given to recognize couples married since the last reception. A young married adult group or the family life committee may host such a reception. Newlyweds from all age groups (including senior adults) will be included.

- Wedding receptions

Except in very small churches, wedding receptions are usually hosted by the bride's family instead of the church. The church hostess or food service director may be asked to plan and cater the reception, however.

- Silver or golden wedding receptions or birthdays of elderly persons

Children of the honorees or Sunday School departments or classes may host silver or golden wedding anniversaries held at the church. In the case of an anniversary of a staff member or other long-time worker in the church, the reception is sometimes given by the church, especially in small churches.

Elderly persons (85, 90, 95, or 100 years of age) may be honored with birthday parties held at the church. The family or class of the honoree, or, occasionally, the church, may host the reception.

THE CHURCH HOSTESS/FOOD SERVICE DIRECTOR AND WEDDING RECEPTIONS

The bride (or her mother) usually needs help. If the church does not have a hostess or food service director on the staff, a committee may be needed to assist with planning wedding receptions.

In some sections of the country, or in some ethnic communities, a picnic-style meal or a formal sit-down dinner are the custom for wedding receptions. A meal is not necessary, however. If the reception comes at mealtime, the bride may wish to serve sandwiches or a salad (such as chicken) in a tart shell; but ordinarily, wedding cake, punch, nuts, and mints are adequate.

Many food services directors prefer to cater the reception themselves. They are familiar with the church equipment and policies and know where to buy supplies to save money. However, if the bride's family prefers to use an outside caterer, the food services director will want to talk personally with the caterer about church policies.

When the food services director talks with the bride's mother, well in advance of the wedding, he will want to discuss the number of guests expected, the amount of nuts and mints needed (usually only about 65 percent of guests take nuts and mints), silver, linens, cups, table arrangements, source of cakes, and other details. Because the food services director has worked with many receptions, he/she will be able to give the bride or her mother a great deal of help. Don't hesitate to offer.

AT HOME

- Honoring a bride-to-be

In some communities, an announcement party is given, usually by the bride's mother, a few months before the wedding. The announcement party is most often a tea or open house. If the party is to include the bride and women friends only, an afternoon tea is usually chosen. If it is to include the groom and both sexes as guests, an evening reception or open house will be scheduled.

In addition to the announcement party, other teas, some with gifts and some without, are often given for brides, with friends as hostesses. Couples sometimes give evening receptions for the bride- and groom-to-be, with both men and women guests.

- Wedding receptions

If the wedding guests can be accommodated in the home of the bride's parents, the reception is sometimes given there. Although not as convenient for the guests as a church reception, the home reception is more personal.

- Honoring newlyweds

A reception may be given to honor a bride and groom after the wedding, especially when one of the couple is from out of town and has not met many friends of the other. If the wedding has been in the bride's hometown, the groom's parents or other friends often give a reception for them the first time they visit the groom's hometown after the wedding.

- Honoring graduates

High school or college graduates may be honored by their parents or other relatives. A tea, reception, or open house is often the chosen kind of party.

- Celebrating a wedding anniversary

A couple may invite their friends to an open house in honor of their own wedding anniversary. Children (grown) or good friends may honor a couple with an open house to celebrate a silver or golden wedding anniversary.

- Celebrating a special birthday

Some birthdays stand out as special—the sixteenth, the twenty-first, the seventy-fifth, and each five years afterward. (Many people do not care to celebrate publicly those between!) Although some sixteens and twenty-ones are more likely to prefer some other kind of party, older persons find a reception or open house to be an ideal way to celebrate a birthday.

- Celebrating a holiday

Although Christmas and New Year's are the most common occasions for a family to choose to have an open house, other holidays may also be occasions for a gathering of friends. A valentine tea for women can be a lovely occasion, or an evening reception can carry out the valentine theme. A harvest theme makes a beautiful setting for a Thanksgiving reception.

- To show off a new home

When a young couple moves into their first home, when a single buys his/her first condo or house, or when the middle-aged or older couple finally builds their dream house—any time there's a new home, there's an occasion to invite friends to share the joy. An open house is in order.

- Honoring special achievements

When a friend writes a book, wins a prize, receives a promotion, wins an election, or is recognized in any way, a family may decide to give a reception to honor him or her. Usually women's parties will be in the afternoon and those for both men and women in the evening, but that is not always the case.

- Introducing newcomers

New neighbors move into the community. To help them become acquainted and feel welcome, a reception may be given in their honor.

- Introducing special guests

When Mom's former college roommate or Uncle Grant and Aunt Martha or Dad's boss from New York comes to town, a family may want their friends to meet the company. An open house, reception, or tea may be the answer.

- Saying thank you to people who have been supportive

Families who have faced difficulties of one kind or another may wish to say thank you to the persons who have helped. Persons in the church who have served as teachers for any member of the family, along with church leaders, may be invited to a home to receive thank you from family members.

RECEPTION, TEA, OR OPEN HOUSE MENUS

Wassail (p. 121)
Butter Cookies (p. 111)
No-Bake Orange Balls (p. 117)
Hot Crabmeat Dip with Crackers (p. 34)

Extra Special Punch (p. 120)
Orange Meltaways (p. 102)
Petit Fours (p. 105)
Mints, Nuts

Walnut Finger Sandwiches (p. 37)
Peanut Butter-Bacon Finger Sandwiches (p. 36)
Nuts
Pecan Tarts (small)
Coffee or Tea

Breakfasts, Brunches, Coffees, Coffee Breaks

In recent years, morning has grown in popularity as a time for entertainment. Both the church and the home become the scene for special occasion breakfast, brunch, coffee, and coffee break occasions.

What's the difference? Breakfast is usually a begin-the-day meal. A brunch, on the other hand, comes later in the morning and usually takes the place of both breakfast and lunch. It may even be as late as noon, with inclusion of traditional breakfast foods making it *brunch* instead of *lunch*.

Coffees are very much like teas, except they are scheduled in the morning. Often both tea and coffee are served. A coffee break, on the other hand, usually comes at a work or meeting break period. The terms *coffee* and *coffee break* are used interchangeably, although a coffee is usually a more formal occasion.

AT CHURCH

A church may have a breakfast on any of these occasions.

- Honoring graduates or new college students

Breakfasts of this nature are usually scheduled on Sunday morning before Sunday School. If high school graduates are being honored, their parents are usually included. In college towns, students may be honored with a breakfast the first Sunday after school starts, giving them an opportunity to meet church leaders.

- Praying together

Saturday morning prayer breakfasts are held in some churches, sometimes before the launching of a new church year, as a part of revival preparation, or in support of a stewardship campaign.

- Celebrating a new year

A breakfast may be held to greet the new year, share resolutions, and make commitments. New Year's breakfasts may be held shortly after midnight, at the normal breakfast time, or later in the morning.

- Fellowshipping before or after Sunday School

In many churches, a monthly or quarterly "feast" is planned before Sunday School, with coffee, juice, and finger foods. Other churches prefer the time between Sunday School and morning worship.

- Honoring New Members

If annual promotion is observed, adult Sunday School departments may welcome those coming in to their department on Promotion Day. The first fifteen or twenty minutes may be used for a time of fellowship, coffee, and goodies.

- Beginning weekday meetings

Women's groups or senior adults often plan coffee as the first item on the agenda for a weekday meeting. The program may follow.

- As a part of Saturday study or work groups

When study or work groups meet on Saturday, a breakfast may begin the meeting. If a breakfast is not scheduled, a mid-morning coffee break will usually be included.

AT HOME

- Celebrating holidays

When members of the family are all at home on holidays, a special breakfast may be a part of the celebration. Whether guests are included should be a family decision. Grandparents are a part of some family celebrations. If grandparents are not available, other senior adults or another person who might be lonely may be included.

- Celebrating birthdays

Some families celebrate birthdays with a special breakfast. If schedules are not too crowded, birthday breakfasts can become special occasions.

- Saying good-bye to friends

If friends are moving or even leaving for an extended trip, they might appreciate a breakfast invitation. Their trip can be celebrated (or their moving mourned if they are leaving town) and they can leave without washing dishes or wondering what to do with the leftover milk.

- Honoring brides, new neighbors, or celebrating special achievements

A brunch or morning coffee is a gracious but not-too-expensive way to honor a friend. Most of the occasions for teas may also be appropriate for coffees.

- Supporting political candidates

Christians need to be involved in politics. Select the candidate you wish to support and invite your friends and neighbors to a Saturday morning coffee to meet him/her.

SPECIAL BREAKFAST MENUS

Special breakfasts, like everyday breakfasts, are an important meal. Protein (milk, meat, eggs, whole-grain cereals) is needed to begin the day. Fruit or fruit juice is important for good nutrition.

Apricot Nectar
Crisp Bacon
Breakfast Bread Pudding (p. 86)

Tomato Juice
Anne's Egg Casserole (p. 57)
Fruit Cup with Mint Dressing (p. 49)
Cherry Blossom Coffee Cake (p. 89)
Hot Tea, Coffee

Half Cantaloupe
Lemon Tea Bread (p. 83)
with Honey and Butter
Scrambled Eggs

Tomato Juice
Tex-Mex Eggs (p. 57)
Marvelous Muffins (p. 85)
Coffee or Milk

Orange Juice
Company Scrambled Eggs (p. 57)
Bacon
Banana Muffins (p. 87) and Butter
Coffee or Milk

Grapefruit Juice
Western Omelette (p. 59)
Baked Cheese Grits (p. 74)
Hot Fruit Compote (p. 81)
Cinnamon-Nut Bread (p. 91)
Coffee, Milk

BRUNCH OR COFFEE MENUS

Hot Fruit Compote
Egg Casserole (p. 55)
Steak and Biscuits (p. 37)
Peanut Sticks (p. 34)
Cinnamon Breadsticks (p. 37)
Cream Wafer Cookies (p. 101)
Coffee or Tea

Hot Chicken Salad Pinwheel (p. 54)
Orange Carrot Salad (p. 51)
Whole Wheat Banana Bread (p. 88)
Fresh Iced Tea

Bacon and Egg Stuffed Tomatoes (p. 81)
Cucumbers in Sour Cream (p. 51)
Banana Muffins (p. 87)
Pineapple Pudding (p. 113)

Fresh Peaches Elegante (p. 94)
Grapefruit Chicken Casserole (p. 58)
Oatmeal Cookies (p. 110)
Cheese Custard Tarts (p. 107)
Coffee or Tea

Pineapple Chicken Salad Pie (p. 47)
Fruit Salad with Poppy Seed Dressing (p. 48)
Feather Biscuits (p. 89)
Strawberry Tarts (p. 110)

Fresh Fruit Cup
Eggs a la King in Sausage Ring (p. 59)
Apricot Coffee Cake (p. 82)
Fresh Apple Bread (p. 83)
Whole Wheat Bread (p. 86) with Butter
Coffee or Tea

Luncheons

Lunch in today's society is usually a light meal. Gone are the days when everyone in the family came home at noon for dinner. There are many advantages in scheduling special occasions at the lunch hour, however, and both home and church can benefit.

AT CHURCH

- Working people's meetings

Work or study groups often meet around the lunch table to conserve time, especially family time. Working men and women may meet for church committee work, Sunday School planning, Bible study, mission study, or other church activities. Their evenings are then free for family time.

- Daytime meetings

People who do not work during the day often prefer that meetings not be held at night. Senior adults may not want to be out at night. Women not employed outside the home prefer daytime to evening meetings to conserve family time and, in an increasing number of communities, because of safety factors. Mission study and mission action groups, Bible study, craft and hobby classes, exercise programs, and prayer groups may be held on weekdays with lunch served.

- Interchurch groups

Frequently churches in the community cooperate in various endeavors that involve daytime meetings and lunch. Pastors' conferences, women's meetings, leader training programs, church staff fellowship and enrichment meetings, and ministers' wives' fellowships often involve luncheons.

AT HOME

Many of the home occasions suggested for dinners may be celebrated with luncheons. When the woman who is not employed outside the home entertains other women, she often chooses a luncheon. Even some women who work are free to attend a class meeting or bridal luncheon in a home.

When the family is home on a holiday or vacation, lunch may be a time for celebration. After-church lunch on Sunday is another possibility if it is kept simple so that the hostess does not find her study and worship distracted by worries about lunch.

- Children's entertaining

Lunch is a happy time for a preschooler to entertain friends. During school vacations, older children, even teenagers, may enjoy having friends visit for an informal luncheon.

MENUS

For Women

Cashew Tuna Casserole (p. 57)
Asparagus Grape Salad (p. 41)
Marvelous Muffins (p. 85)
Pot de Créme (p. 98)
Coffee or Tea

Oven-Barbecued Chicken (p. 54)
Pecan-Stuffed Eggs (p. 51)
Sunny Salad (p. 46)
Carrot Lemon Squares (p. 112)
Blended Iced Tea

Chicken and Sweet Cream Biscuits (p. 57)
Honey Fruit Salad (p. 39)
Crescents (p. 114)
Lemon Ice Cream (p. 111)
Hot Spiced Tea

Salmon Croquettes (p. 60)
Luci Mae's Stuffed Peaches (p. 98)
Buttermilk Pie (p. 104)
Pink Lemonade

Congealed Salmon Salad (p. 42)
Rice-Nut Casserole (p. 68)
Honey Fruit Salad (p. 39)
Assorted Crackers
Peach Melba (p. 93)
Coffee or Tea

Hot Chicken Salad Pinwheel (p. 54)
Orange Carrot Salad (p. 51)
Whole Wheat Banana Bread (p. 88)
Cottage Cheese and Pear
Coffee, Hot Tea

Cold Sliced Ham, Roast Beef, Chicken, or Turkey
English Pea Salad (p. 42)
Peanutty Squash (p. 66)
Whole Wheat Bread (p. 86)
Devil's Food Cupcakes (p. 103)
Coffee or Tea

White Fish in Cheese Sauce (p. 62)
Different Spinach Salad (p. 42)
Cranberry Lemon Nut Bread (p. 87)
Oklahoma Tarts (p. 92)

Salad Bar
Peanut Corn Bread (p. 83)
Choice of Dieter's Choice (p. 92) or Double Good Banana Cake (p. 103)

Dinners and Banquets

AT CHURCH

- Celebrating holidays

Look at almost any church calendar and you will find at least one, and usually more, Valentine banquets. Thanksgiving calls for at least one dinner, and almost every night in December will be the occasion of at least one Christmas banquet. Other holidays need not be left out; any one can be the occasion for a banquet for the entire church or for some group within the church.

- Celebrating anniversaries

The anniversary of the church or the anniversary of a staff member may be celebrated with a banquet.

- A feature of the stewardship campaign

A fellowship dinner is frequently one feature of the church's stewardship campaign. Not only is it a time to promote the budget, but it is a time to foster fellowship within the church membership.

- Honoring graduates

High school or college graduates are often honored with a banquet at the church. The goal is to make the church banquet as nice as or nicer than any other graduation activity. In some communities where a school activity is scheduled that Christian young people may feel is questionable, a banquet at the church becomes an alternative.

- Promoting fellowship within organizational units

The choir, deacons, men's or women's groups, classes or departments, single adults, senior adults, or other groups may have an annual banquet.

- Recognizing leaders

An annual leadership banquet may be a means of saying thank you to officers and/or committees at the end of their term of office—or at the beginning as part of their orientation and training.

- Meeting unchurched persons

Church members may be asked to bring their unchurched neighbors and friends to a banquet to meet church leaders and to learn about the opportunities the church has to offer. Such banquets are particularly appropriate in fast-growing communities.

THE CHURCH HOSTESS/FOOD SERVICE DIRECTOR AND BANQUETS

The church hostess/food service director spends a great deal of time and energy on church banquets. Here are some questions he/she will need to consider:

- What time is best?

What time works best for your church? Naturally, you want the banquet when the guests can come; but, for the kitchen help, the earlier the better. Remember, you'll be paying kitchen help by the hour. Let them go home as early as possible. Six-thirty for appetizer and seven o'clock for the meal may be fine.

- What should the meal cost?

What is affordable? Is the church subsidizing the meal? Will the price keep people away if it is too much? Usually the hostess/food services director will do well to plan several menus, ranging from least expensive to more expensive. Let the group sponsoring the banquet determine which best meets their needs. Some may want to skip an appetizer or serve only one vegetable. Let them decide.

- Who will provide decorations and decorate tables?

(See page 9 for suggestions.) If the cost of decorations must be added to the meal, don't forget to tell the social committee as plans develop.

- Will extra equipment be needed? Do you have enough steam tables, pans, silverware, linens, glassware? Should you borrow from another church, buy, or rent if you do not have enough? Must the rental cost be added to the price of the meal?

- What serving style will be best?

Will people walk through the line, serve themselves from a buffet, or be seated and be served at a table? Consider the style that best displays the food you are serving, is the fastest, and is the most appropriate for the available help. Unless speed is of vital importance, going through the cafeteria line is not best for banquets. Buffet tables, however, can be elegant. If a seated dinner is desired, you may find youth or senior adults who are willing to serve. Enlist enough workers to serve to equal 5 percent of the attendance.

For a buffet, pull out all the stops and really shine! Colors should reign supreme, just as if your table was set for kings. Even the budget buffet can be made to look glamorous. Incorporate as many little extras as the budget will allow. Try such things as whole baked apples with brown sugar-cinnamon glaze; rice casserole with green and red bell peppers and mushrooms, garnished with French-fried onion rings; squash casserole with corn flake topping; three bean salad, colorful and spicy; marinated carrots; broccoli spears with mayonnaise-mustard-lemon sauce; large bottom round of roast garnished with whole crabapples; sliced ham with raisin sauce surrounded by spiced peach halves; large punch bowl full of fresh and canned fruits; green and red whole sweet cherry peppers, and sweet potato casserole with puffy toasted marshmallows. Can you picture it? Try it!

AT HOME

They're banquets if they are at the church, but we usually call them dinner parties if they're in the home. Make them special, however—whether there are guests or not.

- Celebrating birthdays

Every member of every family needs to feel special, loved, and wanted. A special birthday dinner is one way families may show they care. Only the family may be present, or the honoree may choose a friend or friends to be a part of the celebration. (If Mother is the only cook and dishwasher in the family, go out on her birthday! But make the others at-home events.)

- Holidays

Whether there are guests or not, make every holiday a special day for the family. Even Groundhog Day, Arbor Day, and, if you're a Peanuts fan, Beethoven's birthday, can be included in the family's special occasion dinners.

- Entertaining guests

Dinner parties for special guests ought to be a part of every family's calendar of activities. Some will be dinner parties just for Mother and Daddy and their guests, but the whole family can be included in others.

- Celebrations of special achievements

Dad or Mom gets a promotion at work, Johnny makes the debate team, Sis is accepted by the college of her choice, Little Brother is chosen captain of his ball team—these are causes for celebration. A special family dinner may be an appropriate way to celebrate.

- Anniversaries

The anniversary of Mom and Dad's first date, their wedding anniversary, the anniversary of a family member becoming a Christian, the anniversary of the move to the house or town where they now live, or the anniversary of the adoption of a child—these are occasions when families may celebrate with a dinner.

- Family reunions

The extended family may be together seldom; but, when they are, those are special occasions.

21

Grandparents may come for an annual visit, or the entire clan may be together only once a year even when they live in the same town. Make it a special dinner when they come to your home!

• Welcome for new neighbors

A new family on the block or in the church may be invited for a special dinner party to help them feel at home and welcome.

• Outreach/Ministry

A dinner party may be given for an unchurched family to help them become acquainted with church members. Persons who are lonely may be invited, including elderly persons, singles with few friends, internationals far from home, or persons who are bereaved.

Serve a sit-down meal, or let your guests serve themselves from the buffet, a folding table, or the kitchen table. Or you may have room to put up folding tables where your guests will sit to eat, with food on the dining table.

DINNER OR BANQUET MENUS

Tomato Juice
Penny Hors d'oeuvres (p. 34)
Swiss Steak (p. 53)
Honey Wheat Biscuits (p. 84)
Rice-Nut Casserole (p. 68)
Green Bean Salad (p. 39)
Peach Delight (p. 95)
Coffee or Tea

Strawberry-Apple Punch (p. 122)
Beef Stroganoff with Noodles (p. 58)
Grapefruit-Avocado Salad (p. 43)
Broccoli Sesame (p. 67)
Feather Biscuits (p. 89)
Baked Alaska (p. 96) or Chocolate Angel Dessert (p. 98)

Spinach Dip with Crackers (p. 35)
White Fish in Cheese Sauce (p. 62)
Sara Ann's Potatoes (p. 76)
Orange Carrot Salad (p. 51)
Whipped Angel Food Pie (p. 108)

Broccoli Dip (p. 33) with Corn Chips
Chicken Marengo (p. 61)
Special Occasion Potatoes (p. 69)
Limas and Mushrooms (p. 69)
Feather Biscuits (p. 89)
Raspberry Delight (p. 94)

Marinated Pork Roast (p. 64)
Beets and Apples (p. 75)
Green Beans in Sour Cream (p. 77)
Shirley's Spinach Salad (p. 79)
Coconut Cloud (p. 108)

Easy Nachos (p. 33) and Tomato Juice
or Chili Con Queso (p. 36) with Corn Chips
King Ranch Chicken (p. 53)
Lime Gelatin-Avocado Salad (p. 41)
Fried Bananas (p. 70)
Peach Cobbler (p. 106)

Raisin Ham (p. 61)
Fresh Vegetable Marinate (p. 51)
Potatoes Gourmet (p. 73)
Ice Cream Delight (p. 117)

Cranberry Punch (p. 121)
Chicken Parmigiana (p. 62)
Apricot Glazed Carrots (p. 80)
Broccoli-Cheese Delight (p. 76)
Parmesan Tomatoes (p. 80)
Chocolate Mint Cups (p. 110)

Chicken Quiche (p. 58)
Olive Potatoes (p. 77)
Shirley's Spinach (p. 79)
Ambrosia Bowl
Pear Pecan Dessert (p. 104)

Snacks and Refreshments

Often we serve something to eat but not a complete meal. Usually these occasions call for dessert; but, with obesity such a serious problem, other kinds of food will be considered.

AT CHURCH

- After afternoon or evening meetings or social hours

Many church groups serve refreshments after meetings. Class meetings, parent meetings, special choir rehearsals, visitation groups, committee meetings, parties, study groups, or prayer groups often end with a time of refreshment to build group spirit and to help those who are new in the group to become better acquainted.

- In children's groups

Most children eat between meals. If they are in nursery school, kindergarten, or even primary grades, they are accustomed to a midmorning snack at school. When they are at church for as much as two and one-half or three hours, they often become restless and irritable because they are hungry. Simple refreshments (not sweets) are desirable.

AT HOME

- Birthday parties

Instead of celebrating birthdays with a meal, some families prefer to have friends of the honoree in for a party. Refreshments are served.

- Game parties

Many families enjoy games. An evening spent in playing a favorite game may be followed by refreshments. The game party may include only family members, or it may include any member of the family and his/her friends.

- Visiting with friends, relatives, neighbors

Entertaining simply, with informal visitation and dessert, is an inexpensive but satisfying way of hosting. Not only can close friends and extended families be entertained in this manner, but the home may be used as an outreach ministry center by inviting persons in need of friendship and support.

- Entertaining groups in the home

There are many occasions for group meetings to be held in the home, and serving refreshments is a gracious way to promote fellowship and group spirit. Church meetings (such as Sunday School class, Bible study groups, other study groups, prayer groups, visitation groups or mission action groups) may be more convenient and energy saving if held in the home of a member. Civic or political work groups may also meet in the home. Showers for brides or prospective parents are popular home entertainments, as are sales parties for jewelry, household items, or cosmetics.

SNACKS AND REFRESHMENT MENUS

For Children

Peanut Sticks	**Orange Candy Cookies (p. 97)**
Carrott Slices, Apple Slices	**Another Peppermint Punch (p. 123)**
Milk	

For Youth

Saucy Dip (p. 33) with Chips	**Peanut Butter and Crackers**
Easy Nachos (p. 33)	**Celery and Carrot Sticks**
Chili con Queso (p. 36) with Corn Chips	**Apple Slices, Cheese Cubes**
Soft Drinks	**Milk (served in punch bowl)**

Assorted Cheeses and Crackers
Grapes
Fresh Pears, Quartered and Cored
Coffee or Tea

Celery, Carrot Sticks
Broccoli Flowerets, Cauliflower Flowerets
Hot Cheesy Dip (to eat with vegetables) (p. 34)

Fig Preserves Cake (p. 102)
Viennese Coffee (p. 121)

Coconut Custard Pie (p. 104)
Hot Cranberry Punch (p. 121)

Date Crisps (p. 37)
Cinnamon Breadsticks (p. 37)

Meals Away

There's a whole classification of special occasion entertaining that is not held in the church building or in the home. We've chosen to lump these together.

RETREAT MEALS

If the church has a retreat center or has access to other retreat space, retreats are probably scattered throughout the year on the church calendar. You may have youth retreats, choir retreats, staff retreats, church council retreats, marriage enrichment retreats, family enrichment retreats, single adult retreats, senior adult retreats, Sunday School workers retreats, prayer retreats, mission study retreats—almost anything the church does can be done in a retreat setting. Often the food services director or a committee of church members is responsible for the meals. In some instances the retreat center has a kitchen staff, but the group may be asked to plan menus and purchase groceries.

PICNICS

Many churches have an annual all-church picnic. In addition, classes, departments, and many other groups have picnics throughout the year. Picnics may be catered, food may be brought from the church kitchen, or each family or person coming may bring a picnic basket of goodies.

What family does not go on picnics? It may be a bicycle trip to the nearest park to spread a lunch under the trees, or it may be an all-day outing to a wooded or lake area with a refrigerated cooler full of picnic food. It may be just the family, or it may be a reunion of the extended family or friends.

Family or church picnics may be tailgating occasions before ballgames, en route to conventions, or on any trip when a picnic meal is carried from the home.

CAMP-OUT STYLE MEALS

Mission trips are becoming more and more popular with adults as well as youth in many churches. Often two or three persons go along to serve as cooks. They may have a motor home or trailer as their kitchen, or they may cook outside over a grill, with a tent for rainy day protection.

Family camp-out meals may come on family camping trip, on vacation, or on short trips.

MISSION ACTION MEALS

Either church groups or families may take a meal to an individual, a family, or group as a way of saying "I love you." Times of extended illness or bereavement often call for meals to be taken to fellow church members. Disasters such as floods, storms, or fires may call for a church to respond by taking meals to a larger group. A shut-in, in a home or institution, may have a day brightened by having family or friends bring a tray of home-cooked food.

THE CHURCH HOSTESS/FOOD SERVICE DIRECTOR AND THE CHURCH PICNIC

One of the highlights of the church year is the all-church picnic. The picnic is a great time of Christian fellowship, but proper planning and leadership is essential to pulling off the big event!

Get together with the church staff and plan well in advance (six months to a year) the church picnic. At this time some basic principles need to be established and responsibilities assigned. Who is going to plan activities? Who will secure the picnic site—make all the necessary arrangements? What are the food arrangements?—do church members bring all the food? What duties does your food service area need to perform?

If your church has a recreation committee, activities director, or someone in a similar position, assign them (in the proper manner) to the logistics of the picnic—making signs to help people find the picnic site or having individual "picnic guides" stationed at major intersections leading people to the picnic site. These are just two of the many ways you can add personal touches that show you care and are interested in the members' well-being.

While others are busy at work on the nitty-gritty, you need to concentrate on the food. If the situation is normal, most church families bring a complete meal—enough for their family *plus* one. Fried chicken, ham, roast beef, meat casseroles, all sorts of vegetables, assorted salads and tons of desserts. What do you do with it all? You must take charge of the situation before you arrive at the site on Picnic Day. Lay the potential table out mentally and/or physically to see if your ideas and layout will work. Ask another person with expertise in serving to give his/her help.

Checklist for the All-Church Picnic:
  Things we need for the picnic:
    Plastic forks and spoons
    Firm Styrofoam dinner plates
    Good quality dinner napkins
    Extra-large (12-16 oz.) Styrofoam cups
    Plenty of ice
    8' folding tables
    Table cover (plastic or paper)
    Deep steam table pans
    Tongs
    Butcher knives
    Serving spoons and/or tablespoons
    Ice tea concentrate
    Dry drink mix—Fruit Punch, Orange, or Lemonade
    Several large pots for water
    Tea towels/aprons
    Plenty of large trash bags and ties

Some notes

(a) Buy plastic forks and spoons—a good quality. Don't take your stainless flatware—it costs twice the price to replace one piece compared to 100 count of either kind of plastic flatware.

(b) Get large Styrofoam cups—they keep drinks cooler longer, and you won't be bothered with timely refills.

(c) Get the best quality dinner napkin. There is nothing worse than being on a picnic with a flimsy nonabsorbent napkin. The crowd will remember nice little extras like this, and there will be one less "dread" of going to a picnic.

(d) You will need 3 serving tables for each 100 people in attendance—2 deep steam table pans, 2 tongs, 3 butcher knives, plenty of tablespoons. (Suggestion: Use church serving spoons and mark the back side

DRINKS

D
E
S
S
E
R
T
S

BREADS

MEATS

CASSEROLES

VEGETABLES

POTATO CHIPS,
RELISH TRAY, ETC.

SALADS

SPOONS	N A P K I N S	PLATES	N A P K I N S	SPOONS
FORKS		PLATES		FORKS

This is three tables together lengthwise with paper covering
sectioned off with magic marker as shown in diagram.

with red finger nail polish. Tell *everyone* *not* to bring their serving spoons—They only get lost and should someone forget—just look on the back for the unmarked spoon.)

(e) Make up a large amount of tea concentrate. Picnic crowds drink more than usual, so be prepared! By taking tea in a concentrate, there is no hassle with tea shaking and sloshing and spilling on the way. Water should be available nearby to dilute the concentrate.

(f) Make up a couple of flavors of some sort of punch for the young ones and the adults. Adults sometimes prefer a change from the norm. Plan a set amount and don't worry when it's gone. Also, include water as an optional drink.

(g) Take tea towels and aprons for you and your principal workers.

(h) Get your equipment, transportation, people, and any other matters in a time schedule on leaving/arriving/preparation/etc. so everyone will know *what's happening-when*!! Allow ample time (plus) for *every* movement, etc., and be keen to needed or necessary changes.

(i) Take a trial run to the picnic site the day before. Check for cleanliness and access to the areas you need to work in or around. Take a mental picture to see how your table placement will work. Spot where the food line, dessert line, and drink tables will be located.

(j) Call all of your workers two to three days before the picnic and make sure of their plans to help you and the time and place they are to meet.
Good luck and happy picnicking!!

MEALS AWAY ON A TRAY

Lunch or dinner on a tray is a welcome gift for a shut-in. Take a tray for yourself and visit while you both eat. Use a pretty tray cloth and napkin and, if possible, a fresh flower. Make the visit a happy time.

Find out if there are any dietary restrictions. Many persons in nursing homes are on salt-free diets. Use other seasonings to compensate if that is the case. If the patient is not allowed sugar, don't take a dessert and insist "just this once won't hurt!"

TRAY LUNCH

Cinnamon Breadsticks (p. 37) with Cranberry-Apple Juice
Frosted Fruit Salad (p. 40)
Chicken and Sweet Cream Biscuits (p. 57)
Dessert Rice (p. 100)
(If dessert is not permissible, add a green vegetable and use the fruit salad for dessert.)

MEALS AWAY MENUS

Dinner

Oven Barbecued Chicken (p. 54)	**Swiss Steak (p. 53)**
Peanutty Squash (p. 66)	**Brown Rice**
Jalapeno Limas (p. 71)	**Green Bean Casserole (p. 66)**
Tossed Salad	**Second Helping Carrots (p. 68)**
Scalded Corn Cakes (p. 84)	**Marvelous Muffins (p. 85)**
Kid's Delight Pie (p. 93)	**Devil's Food Cupcakes (p. 103)**
Coffee, Tea, or Milk	**Coffee, Tea, or Milk**

Lunch Away

Chicken Quiche (p. 58)
Fruit Cole Slaw (p. 40)
French Bread with Garlic Butter, toasted
Favorite Brownies with Ice Cream Cups
Coffee, Tea, or Milk

Pepperoni Au Gratin
Three Bean Salad
Chess Tarts
Coffee, Tea, or Milk

Breakfast Away

Company Scrambled Eggs (p. 57)
Crisp Bacon
Honey Wheat Biscuits (p. 84)
Coffee, Tea, Milk

Cheddar Slices on Whole Wheat Bread, Toasted
Orange Juice
Coffee, Tea, Milk

Corn Flakes with Vanilla Ice Cream and Fresh Strawberries
Coffee, Tea, Milk

Guides for Buying and Serving in Quantity for the Church

The following is a list of some of the familiar foods used in quantity cooking. The weight is indicated in pounds.

ITEM	SERVINGS		
	25	50	100
Roast beef or pork with little bone	8-10	17-20	35-40
Meat loaf (meat to purchase)	4-5	8-10	17-20
Hamburger steak	5	10	20
Pork chops	8	16	32
Fried chicken	15-20	30-40	60-80
Roast turkey	12-15	25-30	50-60
Chicken (stew or salad)	10-13	20-25	40-50
Cabbage-slaw	5	10	20
Potatoes—white	8	16	32
Potatoes—sweet	10	20	40
Tomatoes, fresh—sliced	7	14	28
Beans, dried	2.5	5	10
Beans, string	8	16	32
English peas, canned or frozen	6	12	24
Rice	2	4	8
Lettuce as a salad (in heads)	4-5	8-10	16-20
Vegetable salad	5 qts.	2.5 gal.	5 gal.
Vegetables and fruits (No. 10 C)	1	2	4

Margarine or butter	¾#	1½#	3#
Ice Cream	1 gal.	2 gal.	4 gal.
Tea	2 oz.	¼#	½#

Coffee: Use ¾-1 lb. and 2½ gal. water for each 55 cups.

Guide to quantity serving—for 50 people

6-8 two-quart casserole dishes, with meat or fish base
6-8 medium size bowls of salad
1 quart salad dressing
5 one-pound loaves sliced bread
6 dozen rolls
7 loaves French bread
5 eight-inch layer cakes
4 oz. bulk tea to 2½ gallons water
12½ quarts sweet milk
2 pounds coffee—when allowing for 2 cups each person
2 pounds cube sugar
1 pound granulated sugar
Coffee cream—2 quarts homogenized milk with two 14½-ounce cans evaporated milk
1½ pounds butter or margarine
1 quart whipping cream, using 1-1½ tablespoons per—
4 No. 3 (46-ounce) cans fruit or vegetable juice for appetizers
5 medium size heads of lettuce for garnishes or salad base
8 medium size heads of lettuce for full salad
3 12-ounce bottles chili sauce to mix with 1 quart mayonnaise for Thousand Island Dressing
15-20 pounds potatoes for mashing

Measurements and Equivalents

Cup Measures

2 cups granulated sugar	1 pound
2¼ cups brown sugar	1 pound
3⅓ cups confectioner's sugar	1 pound
4 cups flour (bread flour)	1 pound
2 cups butter	1 pound
2 cups rice	1 pound
2 cups corn meal	10 ounces
2 cups bread crumbs	8 ounces
2 cups chopped meats, packed	1 pound
2 cups	1 pint
2 pints	1 quart
4 quarts	1 gallon

Other:

2 tablespoons	1 ounce
2 tablespoons	1 fluid ounce
3 teaspoons	1 tablespoon
4 tablespoons	¼ cup
16 tablespoons	1 cup

Relative Proportions of Ingredients

Seasonings:

1 to 2 teaspoons salt to 4 cups flour
1 teaspoon salt to 1 pound meat
1 teaspoon salt to 1 quart water—vegetable cooking

Leavening agents:
2 teaspoons soda to 1 quart milk (sour)
4 to 6 teaspoons baking powder to 4 cups flour

Thickening agents:
Eggs:
4 to 6 eggs—beaten—to 1 quart milk
Flour:
2 tablespoons flour to 1 quart liquid—very thin sauce
4 tablespoons flour to 1 quart liquid—thin soup sauce
6 tablespoons flour to 1 quart liquid for medium sauce
½ cup flour to 1 quart liquid—thick sauce

(All measures are approximate. Use standard measuring cups and spoons.)

Oven Temperatures for Baking and Roasting

Be sure you preheat your oven from 10-15 minutes with the regulator set at the desired temperature.

250° to 275°	**very slow oven**
300°	**slow oven**
325°	**moderately slow oven**
350°	**moderate oven**
375°	**moderately hot oven**
400°	**hot oven**
425°	**very hot oven**

Basic Mixes for Sandwiches (50 servings)

Ham Salad Sandwich: Mix approximately 4 pounds cooked ground ham with grated onion, chopped sweet pickle, and about 2 cups of mayonnaise.

Tuna Fish Sandwich: Combine four or five 13-ounce cans flaked tuna, with chopped sweet pickles, grated onion, 2 tablespoons lemon juice, and 2 cups cooked salad dressing or mayonnaise.

Chicken Salad Sandwiches: Combine 4 pounds cooked chopped or ground chicken meat with ½ cup chopped celery, and 1½ cups mayonnaise for spreading. You may want to add chopped sweet pickles. Add chopped pecans for extra richness.

Bacon and Tomato Sandwiches: You will need 4 pounds of bacon, 7 pounds of ripe sliced tomatoes, 2 heads lettuce, and mayonnaise for spreading. Lay bacon in rows in baking pans; bake until crisp. Drain and place on bread slices which have been spread with mayonnaise. Top with slices of tomatoes and lettuce and another slice of bread. Secure the sandwich with toothpicks.

REQUEST FORM FOR USE OF KITCHEN FACILITY/EQUIPMENT

Date of activity_____Time_____

Name of person making request_____

Group attending activity_____

Expected number in attendance_____

Area of church needed for activity_____

Type of activity_____

_____

Would you like to have kitchen personnel present?_____

Responsibilities:_____

_____

Equipment needed_____

_____

Dry goods needed_____

_____

Other:_____

_____

Budget number (approved) to be charged to_____

_____
Food Service Manager

_____
Person in charge of activity

Recipes

Families, family parties, and church groups come in assorted sizes. Selecting recipes in quantities to fit your family, your dinner party, or your church banquet is not possible.

We have, therefore, a variety. Many recipes are in units of twelve. For a church banquet, you may need to multiply by 20 or 40—or by 2. For the home dinner, you may need to divide by 2 or even by 4.

Other recipes are planned for 4, 6, or 8. We hope arithmetic is one of your best things—or that you have a pocket calculator.

Appetites vary as much as family size. The casserole that serves 8 ladies at a luncheon won't serve 8 teenage boys. The casserole served with baked potatoes and a green vegetable may serve 12, but when served only with a green salad, may serve only 6.

Guides for buying and serving in quantity directly precede this section; remember, these are only guidelines. Practice will help you determine how much to cook for your family or your church group.

Appetizers

SAUCY DIP

½ cup peanut butter
¼ cup mayonnaise
2 to 3 tablespoons milk

1 teaspoon curry powder
Dash of pepper

Blend peanut butter and mayonnaise thoroughly. Gradually stir in milk until dip is of desired consistency. Stir in remaining ingredients. Let stand at least two hours before serving. Serve with potato chips or corn chips.

EASY NACHOS

Jalapeno cheese

Dip-size chips

Slice cheese and cut into pieces slightly smaller than chips. Place a slice of cheese on each chip and stick under the broiler until cheese melts. Serve hot.

BROCCOLI DIP

2 packages frozen chopped broccoli
1 bunch green onions
1 stick margarine or butter
1 roll garlic cheese

¼ teaspoon garlic powder
1 can cream of mushroom soup
Dash Tabasco

Cook broccoli according to package directions. Drain well. Sauté onions in margarine. Add other ingredients and heat over low flame about fifteen minutes. Serve hot with chips.

NEW YEAR'S DIP

4 cups black-eyed peas, cooked and drained
    (canned may be used)
5 jalapeno peppers, chopped
1 tablespoon jalapeno juice
1 large onion, chopped

1 4-ounce can green chilies
1 clove garlic
8 oz. cheddar cheese, grated
8 oz. butter or margarine

Mix peas, pepper, pepper juice, onion, chilies, and garlic in blender. Add some of the juice from peas if needed. Melt cheese and butter and add to the pea mixture. Serve hot with chips.

PEANUT STICKS

Trim crusts from bread (regular slice) and cut into strips. Place on cookie sheet and place in 200° oven for one hour.

In a double boiler, mix ½ cup peanut oil and 1 pound peanut butter. Heat, then dip bread into mixture and roll in crumbs made from bread crusts.

PENNY HORS D'OEUVRES

1 stick butter (room temperature)
½ pound grated cheddar (room temperature)
1 cup flour

½ teaspoon salt
½ package onion soup mix

Cream butter and cheese until well blended. Add other ingredients and mix well. Divide into fourths and form each portion into a roll. Wrap in foil and freeze. When ready to cook, slice thin and place on cookie sheet. Bake in 350° oven for 8 to 10 minutes. Makes about 5 dozen pennies.

HOT CRABMEAT DIP

½ pound Velveeta cheese
½ cup butter or margarine

1 small can crabmeat

Melt cheese and butter in top of double boiler. Stir hard until blended. Mix in drained crabmeat. Serve in chafing dish with crackers.

HOT CHEESY BEEF DIP

⅔ cup chopped pecans
3 tablespoons melted butter or margarine
2 2½-oz. jars dried beef
2 8-oz. packages cream cheese, softened
4 tablespoons milk

½ cup finely chopped green pepper
½ cup finely chopped green onion
2 cloves garlic, pressed
1 teaspoon white pepper
1 cup commercial sour cream

Sauté pecans in butter 3 to 5 minutes; drain on paper towels, and set aside.

Place dried beef in container of electric blender or food processor; chop finely and set aside.

Combine cream cheese and milk in a medium mixing bowl; beat on medium speed of electric mixer until smooth. Stir in beef, green pepper, onion, garlic, and white pepper, mixing well. Stir in sour cream; spoon into a greased 1-quart casserole. Sprinkle pecans on top; bake at 350° for 25 minutes. Serve dip hot with assorted crackers. Makes about 4 cups.

CURRY BACON DIP

1 8-oz. package cream cheese, whipped
2 teaspoons curry powder

4 slices bacon, cooked, drained, and
crumbled

Combine and chill. Makes about one cup.

HOT SHRIMP DIP

1 can cream of shrimp soup
1-5 oz. can shrimp, rinsed well
1-4 oz. can mushrooms, cut into pieces and drained
1 tablespoon Parmesan cheese

1 teaspoon Worcestershire sauce
1 tablespoon chopped parsley
4-8 oz. package cream cheese
Paprika

Mix all ingredients together. Heat in saucepan. Serve in small fondue pot with melba rounds.

VEGETABLE DIP

16-oz. package cream cheese
1 clove garlic, crushed
1 cup sour cream
1 teaspoon Worcestershire

1 teaspoon salt
2 teaspoons lemon juice
⅓ to ½ oz. of 4-oz. package blue cheese

Combine all ingredients. Blend until smooth.

SPINACH DIP

2 10-oz. packages frozen chopped spinach
2 cups mayonnaise
2 cups commercial sour cream

2 medium onions, chopped
2 8-oz. cans water chestnuts, chopped
2 1⅝-oz. packages vegetable soup mix

Thaw spinach; place on paper towels, and press until barely moist.

Combine spinach, mayonnaise, sour cream, onion, water chestnuts, and vegetable soup mix; stir well. Cover and chill mixture several hours. Makes 6 cups. Serve dip with crackers or raw vegetables.

HOT CHICKEN DIP

2 10¾-oz. can cream of mushroom soup, undiluted
2 8-oz. packages cream cheese
2 5-oz. cans chunk white chicken
2 2¾-oz. packages slivered almonds

2 2-oz. cans sliced mushrooms, drained
1 teaspoon Worcestershire sauce
¼ teaspoon garlic powder
¼ teaspoon pepper

Combine all ingredients in a 1-quart saucepan or fondue pot. Cook over medium heat, stirring often, until blended and heated thoroughly. Makes 7 cups. Serve dip hot with chips.

CHEESE AND OLIVE PUFFS

2 cups (½ lb.) grated sharp cheese
½ cup soft butter
1 cup sifted flour

½ teaspoon salt
1 teaspoon paprika
50 stuffed olives

Blend cheese and butter; add flour and dry ingredients. Mix well. Wrap each olive with about 1 teaspoon of mixture. Cover completely and make into a ball. Bake 15 minutes at 400°. Serve hot.

These can be frozen before baking.

WATER CHESTNUT DIP

1 8-oz. carton commercial sour cream
1 cup mayonnaise
2 8-oz. cans water chestnuts, drained and finely
   chopped

¼ cup chopped onion
¼ cup chopped fresh parsley
¾ teaspoon soy sauce
½ teaspoon salt

Combine all ingredients in a medium bowl; stir well. Chill. Makes about 3 cups. Serve dip with potato chips or crackers.

CHICKEN LIVER AND BACON ROLL-UPS

1 pound chicken livers
3 tablespoons Dijon mustard

10 to 12 slices bacon, cut in half
½ cup cracker crumbs

Dip chicken livers lightly in mustard. Wrap a half-slice of bacon around each, and secure with a toothpick; coat livers with crumbs. Makes 6 to 8 appetizer servings. Place in an 8-inch square baking dish; bake at 425° for 25 minutes.

CHILI CON QUESO

1 can cheddar cheese soup
1 4-oz. can green chilies, chopped
1 teaspoon Worcestershire sauce

½ teaspoon Tabasco sauce
½ clove garlic, minced

Mix all ingredients together and heat in double boiler. Keep warm in chafing dish. Serve as dip with corn chips.

VEGETABLE DIP

1 bunch green onions
2 3-oz. packages cream cheese
⅓ cup finely grated carrots

⅓ cup finely grated radishes
⅓ cup finely chopped green pepper
Mayonnaise

Soften cream cheese. Blend in mayonnaise. Add vegetables. More mayonnaise may be added for right consistency. Serve with carrots, celery, cauliflower, or broccoli as "dippers."

CHEESE LOG

1 pound sharp cheddar cheese, grated
3-oz. package cream cheese
1 clove garlic (more or less to taste)

½ cup chopped walnuts or pecans
½ cup freeze-dried chives
Paprika

Mix ingredients well and shape into log. Roll in paprika. Chill and slice. Serve with crackers.

PEANUT BUTTER-BACON FINGER SANDWICHES

Fry bacon until crisp. Drain well, and crumble into crunchy peanut butter. Spread on bread which has been lightly buttered and trimmed. Cut into finger sandwiches.

CINNAMON BREADSTICKS

1 package breadsticks
¼ cup butter

½ cup sugar
1 teaspoon cinnamon

Melt the butter and pour over the breadsticks, being sure that all are covered. Remove from butter and roll in sugar-cinnamon mixture. Place on a cookie sheet and bake for 10 minutes in a 350° oven.

WALNUT FINGER SANDWICHES

Chop English walnuts finely. Mix with softened sweet cream butter and spread on fresh white bread with crusts removed. Cut into finger sandwiches.

STEAK AND BISCUITS

Make small-sized biscuits by your favorite recipe. Break open and butter while hot.

Fry minute steaks or other thin-sliced steak and season with a light dusting of garlic powder. Cut into small pieces and serve in biscuits. Serve hot.

DATE CRISPS

1 box pitted dates

Bacon

Wrap each date with enough bacon to cover. Secure with toothpick; then fry in hot fat until bacon is crisp. Serve hot.

PARMESAN-CARAWAY APPETIZERS

2 cups biscuit mix
1 cup grated Parmesan cheese
⅓ cup milk
1 tablespoon caraway seed
1 tablespoon parsley flakes

2 tablespoons vegetable oil
½ teaspoon garlic powder
½ teaspoon salt
1 egg

Heat oven to 425°. Mix all ingredients until stiff dough forms. Drop by slightly rounded teaspoons about 1 inch apart onto ungreased cookie sheet. Bake until light brown—about 8 minutes. Makes 3 dozen.

RIBBON SANDWICH LOAF

1 loaf unsliced white bread
1 loaf unsliced whole wheat bread
½ cup cream cheese

½ ounce chopped pimento
6 scoops chicken salad filling
12 scoops egg salad

Freeze unsliced bread overnight. When partially defrosted, trim off outside crusts. Slice each loaf lengthwise, five slices from each loaf. Alternate white and dark slices. Spread first layer with egg salad filling (3 scoops); second layer with cream cheese and chopped pimento; third layer with chicken salad filling (3 scoops); and fourth layer with egg salad filling (3 scoops). Spread outside of loaf with plain cream cheese. Chill before slicing.

MAYONNAISE CHEESE PUFFS

1 egg white	¼ teaspoon onion salt
½ cup mayonnaise	1 teaspoon dry mustard
¼ cup grated Parmesan cheese	Crackers or melba toast

Beat egg white until stiff, shiny peaks form. Fold in remaining ingredients. Spread on crackers or toast and place under preheated broiler until puffy and golden brown. Serve immediately. Makes about 20.

TUNA PUFFS

1 egg white	½ can (7 oz.) tuna, drained and flaked
1 cup mayonnaise	24 crackers or toast rounds
¼ teaspoon Worcestershire	

Beat egg white until stiff and fold in mayonnaise, Worcestershire, and tuna. Place crackers on ungreased cookie sheet and drop tuna mixture on them. Broil 1 or two minutes, or until puffed. Makes 24.

Salads

GREEN BEAN SALAD

2 cups cooked green beans (fresh or frozen)
1 avocado, chopped
2 pimientos, chopped
1 medium onion, chopped

⅛ teaspoon garlic salt
⅛ teaspoon pepper
French or Italian dressing

Drain beans; mix with remaining ingredients. Chill. Serves 5.

HONEY FRUIT SALAD

3 cups diced pineapple, apple, pears, or other fruit,
    drained
3 tablespoons honey

½ teaspoon salt
1 cup sour cream
1 cup miniature marshmallows

Mix ingredients and chill before serving.

CARL'S PERFECT POTATO SALAD

5 medium-sized potatoes, boiled
5 eggs, hard cooked
5 small dill pickles
4-ounce jar diced pimientos
1 cup chopped celery

½ cup sliced ripe olives
½ cup chopped green onions
1 tablespoon prepared mustard
Mayonnaise

Peel and dice cold potatoes and eggs. Chop pickles. Add other ingredients except mustard and mayonnaise. Mix mustard and mayonnaise and add last. Keep refrigerated until ready to serve. Serves 6-8.

GREEN PEA SALAD

1 can green peas (15-oz.)
1 small onion, minced
¼ cup chopped celery
½ cup farmer's cheese, diced

½ cup pecan pieces
2 hard-cooked eggs, chopped
½ cup mayonnaise
¼ teaspoon garlic salt

Combine all ingredients and toss with mayonnaise. Serve on lettuce.

FROSTED FRUIT SALAD

1 envelope plain gelatin
¼ cup cold water
1 cup orange juice
1 6½-oz. bottle Dr. Pepper
¾ cup crushed pineapple (unsweetened), drained

¾ cup orange sections, seeds,
    membrane, and pits removed
½ cup pitted dark cherries, drained
3 oz. cream cheese
3 tablespoons lemon juice

Soften gelatin in cold water. Heat orange juice; add gelatin and stir until dissolved. Add Dr. Pepper and blend. Cool until thick; then stir in fruits. Turn into mold and chill until set. Turn out on lettuce on serving dish and frost with cream cheese-lemon juice mixture. Serves 6-8.

RED, WHITE, AND BLUE SALAD

Fresh pineapple, cut into spears
Fresh blueberries, washed and stemmed
Bananas

Fresh strawberries, washed and
    stemmed

Cover serving bowl or platter with lettuce. Arrange fruit attractively on lettuce and pour poppy seed dressing over it.

POPPY SEED DRESSING

¾ cup sour cream
3 tablespoons honey

1 tablespoon lemon juice
1 tablespoon poppy seed

Mix and chill. Makes 1 cup.

FRUIT COLE SLAW

2 bananas, sliced
1 cup unsweetened pineapple chunks, drained
1 cup tart apples, diced
2 cups shredded cabbage
½ cup mayonnaise

¾ teaspoon salt
½ teaspoon sugar or sugar substitute
2 tablespoons vinegar
Dash of paprika, pepper

Combine mayonnaise, vinegar, pepper, paprika, sugar, and salt. Place in a jar and shake well to blend. Pour over fruit and cabbage and toss. 6 servings.

WILTED SPINACH SALAD

6 cups spinach, torn in bite-size pieces
¼ cup sliced green onions
4 hard-cooked eggs, chopped
6 slices bacon

¼ cup vinegar
2 tablespoons water
2 tablespoons sugar or sugar substitute
¼ teaspoon pepper

Combine spinach, onions, and eggs in bowl. Cook bacon until crisp. Crumble. Add vinegar, water, sugar, and pepper to bacon drippings. Bring to boil, stirring constantly. Pour over spinach mixture and toss. Sprinkle with bacon crumbs. Serves 8.

APPLE, CELERY, AND PEA SALAD

4 large tart apples, peeled, cored, and diced
2 9-oz. packages frozen small peas
1½ cups celery, chopped

¼ cup chopped green onions
½ cup mayonnaise
1 tablespoon frozen orange juice
concentrate

Pour lemon juice over apples as soon as they are diced to prevent discoloration. Drain and combine with peas (thawed), celery, and onions. Mix orange juice concentrate with mayonnaise and mix with salad. Serve on lettuce or other greens.

ASPARAGUS GRAPE SALAD

2 9-oz. packages frozen asparagus spears
1 package unflavored gelatin, softened in 1/2 cup
cold water
1½ cups condensed chicken broth

2 cups seedless grapes, rinsed, drained,
and dried
1 cup diced celery

Cook asparagus according to package directions. Drain, reserving liquid. Pour cold water over asparagus for 1 minute, then drain and dry. To ½ cup of the hot asparagus water, add gelatin, stirring until it is dissolved. Then add broth. Chill until it begins to thicken.

When broth mixture is ready to set, arrange the asparagus, grapes and celery in a mold or $8 \times 8 \times 2$ inch dish. Pour gelatin mixture over vegetables and chill for at least three hours. Unmold or cut into squares and serve on lettuce.

LIME GELATIN-AVOCADO SALAD

1 box lime gelatin (3 oz.)
½ teaspoon salt
Juice of 2 lemons
1 ripe avocado
2 tablespoons finely chopped onion

1 15¼-oz. can crushed pineapple in its
own juice
½ cup mayonnaise
½ cup water
1 3-oz. package Philadelphia cream
cheese whipped with ½ cup cream

Boil water and ½ cup juice from pineapple and pour over jello.

Add lemon juice and salt. Let this gel.

Then whip until fluffy and fold in diced avocado, pineapple (drained), cream, onion, and salad dressing. Pour into 8-10 individual molds or one large mold.

RASPBERRY SOUR CREAM SALAD

2 medium bananas
1 small can crushed pineapple, drained
1 12-oz. package frozen raspberries, drained

1 3-oz. package raspberry gelatin
1 cup sour cream
1 cup hot water

Mash bananas. Fold in pineapple and thawed raspberries. Dissolve gelatin in hot water. Fold into fruit mixture and pour half the mixture into mold and refrigerate. When set, spread sour cream over top. Fold remaining mixture on top of sour cream. Return to refrigerator until set. Serves 9.

MOUSSE CUCUMBER

1 large cucumber, sliced thin
1 3-oz. package lime gelatin
⅔ cup boiling water

¼ cup lemon juice
2 tablespoons grated onion
1 cup sour cream

Layer cucumber slices in a bowl, sprinkling each layer lightly with salt. Refrigerate overnight; then drain and dry each cucumber slice with paper towel. Dissolve gelatin in boiling water and add lemon juice. Let cool; then add onion, sour cream, and cucumber. Pour into mold and refrigerate overnight. Unmold and serve on lettuce.

CONGEALED BROCCOLI SALAD

1 envelope gelatin
1 can condensed consommé
¾ cup mayonnaise
4 tablespoons Worcestershire
2 tablespoons lemon juice

¼ teaspoon Tabasco
2 packages frozen chopped broccoli,
    cooked according to directions
4 hard-cooked eggs

Soften gelatin in cold water and dissolve in heated consommé. Add other ingredients except broccoli and eggs, and mix well. Arrange sliced eggs and broccoli in ring mold and pour gelatin mixture over it. Serve on lettuce, with mayonnaise if desired. Serves 6-8.

CONGEALED SALMON SALAD

1 envelope gelatin
1 can tomato soup (condensed)
1 8-oz. package cream cheese
2 tablespoons green onions, chopped

1 cup celery
16-oz. can salmon, flaked
1 cup mayonnaise

Dissolve gelatin in tomato soup over hot water in double boiler. Add cream cheese to soup mixture. Dice celery. Add onion, celery, salmon, and mayonnaise to soup mixture. Mix well, mold, and chill.

JUANITA'S ENGLISH PEA SALAD

1 large head lettuce, torn apart
1 #2 can English peas (small, fancy peas better)
1 4-oz. can sliced water chestnuts

½ cup mayonnaise
½ cup grated Parmesan cheese
2 teaspoons sugar or sugar substitute

Tear lettuce into large salad bowl. Add green peas and water chestnuts. Toss. Cover top with mayonnaise; sprinkle on sugar and cheese. Refrigerate for up to 24 hours. Keeps well if covered. Toss before serving.

DIFFERENT SPINACH SALAD

1 pound fresh spinach
1 onion, minced
2 cups yogurt
¼ teaspoon pepper

2 cloves garlic, crushed
1 teaspoon fresh or dried mint leaves,
    crushed
2 tablespoons chopped peanuts

Stem spinach and break leaves into bite-sized pieces. Combine with onion. Combine yogurt, pepper, and garlic. Toss spinach-onion mixture with yogurt, mint leaves, and peanuts. 4 servings.

GRAPEFRUIT-AVOCADO SALAD

Grapefruit sections

Avocado sliced and dipped in lemon juice

French dressing

Lettuce

Alternate slices of avocado with grapefruit sections on lettuce. Serve with French dressing.

SAVORY TOMATO SALAD

1¼ pounds lemon jello

1½ quarts tomatoes, canned, heated to lukewarm

1 quart cucumbers, grated

¾ cup green peppers, finely chopped

3 tablespoons onions, finely chopped

3 oz. vinegar

3 tablespoons horseradish, prepared

1 oz. salt

1 quart mayonnaise

Dissolve jello in heated tomatoes. Add cucumber, green peppers, onion, vinegar, horseradish, and salt. Chill. When slightly thickened, fold in mayonnaise. Turn into individual molds, or pour into pans. Chill until firm. Unmold on crisp lettuce, romaine, or chicory. Makes 32 servings of 4 ounces each.

UNDER THE SEA SALAD

2 pounds canned pears, diced

9 oz. lime gelatin

1 teaspoon salt

1 pint boiling water

2 pints pear syrup

2 tablespoons vinegar

½ teaspoon ground ginger

2 pounds cottage cheese

Salad greens as needed

Drain canned pears; save syrup for part of liquid in recipe. Dissolve gelatin and salt in boiling water; stir until gelatin is thoroughly dissolved. Add vinegar and pear syrup to gelatin. Fill individual mold or shallow pan half-full of gelatin mixture; refrigerate until firm. Chill remaining gelatin until partially thickened. Add ginger, cottage cheese, and diced pears to partially thickened gelatin. Spread cheese and gelatin mixture over firm gelatin in individual molds or shallow pan. Chill until completely firm. Prepare salad greens according to general directions and arrange on salad plates. Unmold gelatin on crisp greens. Garnish with canned sliced pears, cottage cheese, rosettes of mayonnaise, and maraschino cherries. Makes 20 servings of 4 ounces each.

CRUNCHY HOT CHICKEN SALAD

9 cups diced cooked chicken

3 cups finely chopped celery

2 tablespoons chopped onion

1½ cups sliced almonds

3 10¾ oz. cans cream of chicken soup, undiluted

4½ cups cooked rice

3 tablespoons lemon juice

1½ teaspoons salt

¾ teaspoon pepper

2¼ cups mayonnaise

¾ cup water

9 hard-cooked eggs, sliced

6 cups crushed potato chips

2¼ cups shredded cheddar cheese

Combine first 9 ingredients; toss gently and set aside.

Combine mayonnaise and water; beat with a wire whisk until smooth. Pour over chicken mixture; stir well. Add eggs, and toss gently. Spoon into a greased shallow steam table pan; cover and refrigerate 8 hours or overnight.

Bake at 450° for 10 to 15 minutes or until thoroughly heated. Sprinkle with potato chips and cheese; bake an additional 5 minutes. Makes 18-24 servings.

COLD PLATE - FRUIT, AVOCADO, AND MELON BALLS

INGREDIENTS	AMOUNT	
Grapefruit sections	6 each	1. lettuce
Avocado slices	3 each	2. watermelon balls
Cantaloupe balls	6 each	cantaloupe balls
Watermelon balls	6 each	3. grapefruit section
Orange sections	5 each	avocado slices
Apple slices	½ apple	4. apple slices
Lettuce	⅛ head	orange sections
Cottage Cheese	#40 scoop	5. cottage cheese

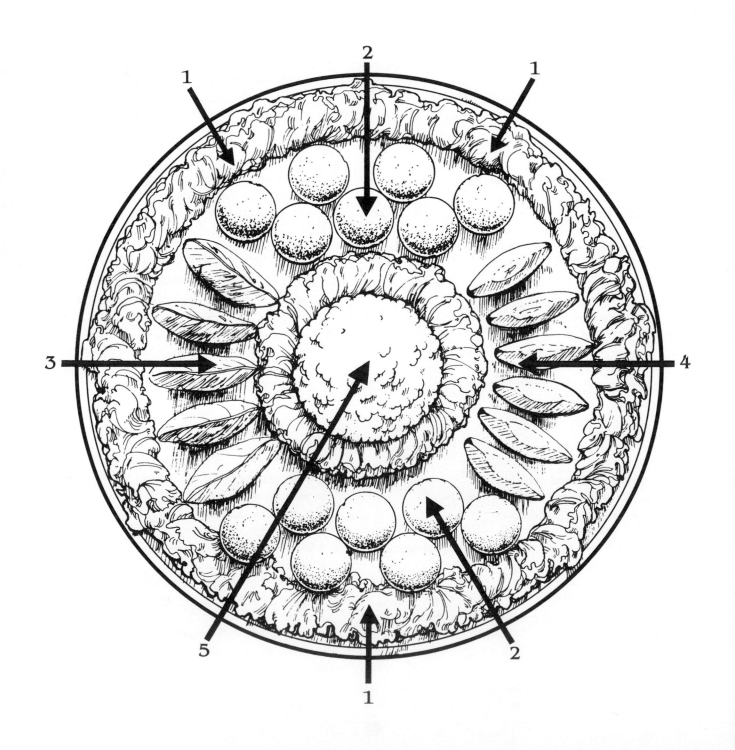

HAWAIIAN SALAD

2½ pounds lime jello
1½ quarts boiling water
2 quarts plus one cup cold water
2 tablespoons salt
4 quarts pineapple, crushed, undrained

1 quart lemon juice
2 quarts celery, diced fine
½ cup pimiento, chopped fine
2 pounds American cheese
½ cup green pepper

Dissolve jello in boiling water; add cold water. Add salt. Add crushed pineapple and lemon juice; then cool. When mixture begins to thicken, fold in celery, pimiento, green pepper, and cheese. Makes 100 servings of 4 ounces each.

SUNSET SALAD

3½ cups lemon gelatin
2 teaspoons salt
1 gallon hot water
½ cup vinegar

2½ quarts grated carrots
1 quart crushed pineapple, canned
1 cup chopped nuts

Dissolve gelatin and salt in hot water. Add vinegar and chill until slightly thickened. Fold in carrots, pineapple, and pecans. Pour into individual molds, shallow pans, or two 3-quart molds. Chill until firm. Unmold or cut into squares. Serve on crisp lettuce with mayonnaise, if desired. Makes 48 portions. Note: Chill large molds 8 hours or overnight. One ½-cup portion provides ¼-cup vegetable.

TROPICAL AMBROSIA

3½ cups orange gelatin
1 teaspoon salt
3¼ quarts hot water
2 tablespoons orange rind, grated

1½ quarts orange sections, drained
1½ quarts crushed pineapple
2 cups flaked coconut

Dissolve gelatin and salt in hot water. Chill until slightly thickened. Add remaining ingredients. Pour into individual molds, shallow pans, or two 3-quart molds. Chill until firm. Unmold or cut in squares. Serve as a salad with salad dressing or as a dessert with custard sauce, if desired. Makes 48 portions.

ASPARAGUS MOLD

4 teaspoons unflavored gelatin
2 cups cold water
4 3-oz. packages lemon-flavored gelatin
8 chicken bouillon cubes
4 cups boiling water
2 cups commercial Green Goddess dressing
4 tablespoons lemon juice

4 14½-oz. cans cut asparagus, drained
2 cups diced celery
8 tablespoons finely chopped green
   pepper
Lettuce leaves (optional)
Mayonnaise

Soften unflavored gelatin in cold water; set aside.

Dissolve lemon-flavored gelatin and bouillon in boiling water; add softened gelatin, stirring until dissolved. Add Green Goddess dressing and lemon juice, stirring with a wire whisk until smooth. Chill until slightly thickened.

Stir asparagus, celery, and green pepper into gelatin mixture. Pour into a lightly oiled mold, and chill salad until firm.

Unmold on lettuce leaves, and garnish with a dollop of mayonnaise, if desired.

CUCUMBER COMBINATION SALAD

20-24 medium-sized cucumbers
6-8 fresh tomatoes, diced
6 onions, sliced thin
Salt

1½ cups white vinegar
1 cup sugar
½ cup salad oil

Peel and slice the cucumbers into cold salted water; use about 1½ teaspoons salt for each quart of water, and have enough water to cover them. Chill for 2 or 3 hours. When ready to prepare salad, drain and rinse the cucumbers and combine with all other ingredients. Toss lightly.

Lift the salad out of the liquid and serve in lettuce cup or in small bowls garnished with lettuce. Makes 50 servings.

Variations:
   Omit the oil and vinegar dressing and substitute 1 quart of mayonnaise.
   To make *Cauliflower Combination Salad* omit the cucumbers and substitute 8 pounds fresh, crisp cauliflower.

CHICKEN-AVOCADO SALAD

4 medium-sized ripe avocados, peeled and cubed
6-12 tablespoons lemon or lime juice
1 tablespoon + 1 teaspoon salt
4 3.5-oz. cans pitted ripe olives, drained and sliced
16-25 stalks celery, chopped (about 8 cups)
8 cups diced cooked chicken

2 cups mayonnaise
4 tablespoons lemon or lime juice
Lettuce leaves
12 hard-cooked eggs, quartered
Pimiento strips

Sprinkle avocado with 6-12 tablespoons lemon juice and salt; toss well. Combine avocado, olives, celery, and chicken; stir gently. Combine mayonnaise and 4 tablespoons lemon juice; mix well. Stir mayonnaise mixture into chicken mixture. Serve salad on lettuce; garnish with egg quarters and pimiento strips. Makes 24 servings.

SPICED APPLE SALAD

50 cooking apples
8 pounds granulated sugar
4 quarts water

1 cup vinegar
2 teaspoons red coloring
2 oz. stick cinnamon

Core, peel, and cut apples in half crosswise. Place apples in flat pan. Prepare the syrup from the above ingredients. Boil syrup one minute. Pour over apples. Bake at 375° for one hour. Watch closely so that apples do not become mushy. Turn apples over after removing from oven if syrup has not covered apples. Refrigerate overnight in syrup. Serve chilled rings on green leafy lettuce. Dot with mayonnaise. Makes 100 servings.

SUNNY SALAD

6 heads bibb lettuce, torn
3 16-oz. cans grapefruit sections, drained
3 16-oz. cans prune plums, drained, pitted and halved

6 bananas, sliced
¾ cup chopped pecans or walnuts

Combine all ingredients in a large bowl. Toss lightly with desired dressing. Makes 24 servings.

PINEAPPLE-CHICKEN SALAD PIE

4 20-oz. cans pineapple chunks, drained
12 cups diced cooked chicken
4 cups chopped celery
1 cup finely chopped green onion
8 tablespoons lemon juice

6-8 teaspoons seasoned salt
1 cup chopped cashew nuts
2 cups mayonnaise
3 baked 9-inch pastry shells, cooled

Combine half of pineapple chunks and next 7 ingredients; stir well. Spoon salad into pastry shells, pressing firmly. Garnish with remaining pineapple chunks; chill before serving. Makes 24 servings. (Note: Pastry shell may be omitted; salad may be served on lettuce leaves if desired.)

MINTED MELON ASPIC

13 oz. lime-flavored gelatin
¼ teaspoon salt
½ cup mint leaves (chopped)
2 quarts boiling water

1 quart honeydew melon balls (medium-
    sized)
Whipped topping (as needed)
Salad greens (as needed)

Combine gelatin, salt, and chopped mint leaves. Add boiling water to gelatin mixture. Stir until gelatin is dissolved. Let stand until cool. Strain. Refrigerate gelatin mixture until partially set. Add melon balls to partially set gelatin. Portion out into individual molds or place in shallow pan. Refrigerate until firm. Prepare salad greens and place on salad plates. Unmold minted melon aspic on crisp greens. Garnish with rosettes of whipped topping and/or melon balls and fresh strawberries. Makes 25 servings of 4 ounces each.

CREAMY PEA SALAD

6 10 oz. packages frozen green peas, thawed
1½ cups chopped onion
1½ cups chopped celery
1½ teaspoons salt
¾ teaspoon pepper

¾ teaspoon whole basil leaves
3 cups commercial sour cream
54 slices bacon, cooked and crumbled
3 cups cashews, coarsely chopped
Lettuce leaves

Combine first 7 ingredients, stirring gently. Chill 3 to 4 hours. Stir in bacon and cashews; serve on lettuce leaves. Makes 24 servings.

MIXED GREEN SALAD WITH CHICKEN

3 cups mayonnaise
¾ cup tarragon vinegar
3 1-oz. packages anchovy fillets, chopped
¾ cup chopped fresh parsley
6 tablespoons chopped green onion
6 tablespoons chopped chives
1½ teaspoons dry mustard

¾ teaspoon salt
1½ small heads iceberg lettuce, torn
12-15 endive leaves, torn
3 heads bibb lettuce, torn
1½ heads romaine, torn
9 cups chopped cooked chicken
6 medium tomatoes, sliced

Combine first 8 ingredients, mixing well. Refrigerate several hours.

Combine salad greens and chicken; toss with dressing. Line a large salad bowl with the tomato slices; fill with salad. Serve immediately. Makes 18-24 servings.

BLACK-EYED PEA SALAD

6 15-oz. cans black-eyed peas, drained
1½ cups chopped red onion
1½ cups chopped green pepper
1½ cloves garlic
¾ cup vinegar

¾ cup sugar
¾ cup vegetable oil
1½ teaspoons salt
Dash of pepper
Dash of hot sauce

Combine first 4 ingredients; toss lightly. Combine remaining ingredients; mix well and pour over pea mixture. Cover and refrigerate at least 12 hours. Remove garlic before serving. Makes 18-24 servings.

LIME SHERBET SALAD

3 8-oz. cans crushed pineapple
3 3-oz. packages lime-flavored gelatin
3 cups lime sherbet

3 fresh pears, peeled and diced
3 cups chopped pecans

Drain pineapple, reserving juice; add enough water to juice to make 3 cups liquid. Bring juice to a boil; add gelatin, stirring to dissolve. Stir in sherbet. Add pineapple, pear, and pecans; mix well, and pour into 3 lightly oiled 6-cup molds. Makes 18-24 servings.

FRUIT SALAD WITH POPPY SEED DRESSING

3 11-oz. cans mandarin oranges, drained
6 apples, cored and chopped
3 pints fresh strawberries, halved
6 bananas, sliced
3-6 avocados, peeled and chopped
1½ cups chopped dates
1 cup orange juice

1 cup vegetable oil
¾ cup honey
1 tablespoon lemon juice
3 tablespoons poppy seeds
1½ teaspoons salt
1½ teaspoons prepared mustard

Combine first 6 ingredients in a large mixing bowl.

Combine remaining ingredients, mixing well. Pour over fruit, and toss gently to coat; chill 1 to 2 hours. Makes 18-24 servings.

CREAMY POTATO SALAD

18 medium potatoes
6 hard-cooked eggs
1⅓ cups mayonnaise
2 teaspoons prepared mustard
1½ cups commercial sour cream
2 teaspoons salt

½ teaspoon pepper
22 slices bacon
½ cup chopped green onion
1 cup chopped celery
½ cup commercial Italian salad
        dressing

Cook potatoes in boiling salted water about 30 minutes, or until tender. Drain well, and cook slightly. Peel and cut potatoes into ¾-inch cubes.

Remove yolks from eggs and mash; set whites aside. Stir mayonnaise, mustard, sour cream, salt, and pepper into yolks; set aside.

Cook bacon until crisp; drain on paper towels, and crumble.

Chop egg whites; add bacon, potatoes, onion, celery, and Italian dressing. Fold in mayonnaise mixture; chill at least 2 hours. Makes 24 servings.

VANILLA FRUIT CUP

1 cup sugar
4 to 8 tablespoons light brown sugar
1 cup water
1 cup orange juice

3 teaspoons vanilla extract
16 cups assorted fresh fruit (melon balls,
  strawberries, peach slices, green
  grapes, and banana slices)

Combine first 5 ingredients in a medium saucepan. Bring to a boil; reduce heat, and simmer 5 to 8 minutes. Remove from heat, and stir in vanilla. Arrange fruit in a large bowl; pour syrup over fruit and toss gently. Chill several hours or overnight. Makes 24 servings.

FRUIT CUP WITH MINT DRESSING

3 cantaloupes, peeled, seeded, and cut into bite-
  sized pieces
3 cups cubed honeydew melon
3 cups cubed watermelon

3 cups green grapes
3 cups fresh strawberries
1 cup sliced fresh peaches
Mint Dressing

Combine fruit in a large bowl; cover tightly, and chill. Makes 24-30 servings. Serve with Mint Dressing.

MINT DRESSING

3 8-oz. cartons commercial sour cream
3 to 6 tablespoons chopped fresh mint or mint
  extract to taste

6 tablespoons powdered sugar
¾ teaspoon ground cardamom
3 drops green food coloring (optional)

Combine all ingredients; mix well. Cover and chill for at least 30 minutes. Makes 3 cups.

DILLY DRESSING

1 medium onion, finely chopped
¾ cup vegetable oil
½ cup catsup
½ cup sugar
¼ cup vinegar

¼ cup water
1 teaspoon dillweed
½ teaspoon salt
¼ teaspoon paprika

Combine all ingredients in container of electric blender; blend well. Chill. Serve dressing over salad greens. Makes about 2½ cups.

RUSSIAN MAYONNAISE

6 hard-cooked egg yolks
3 teaspoons salt
⅜ teaspoon freshly ground pepper
3 teaspoons dry mustard
3 teaspoons sugar

4½ cups commercial sour cream
¼ cup olive oil
3 teaspoons lemon juice
3 tablespoons vinegar

Press egg yolks through a sieve; add salt, pepper, dry mustard, sugar, and sour cream, mixing well. Add oil in a slow, steady stream, stirring constantly. Add lemon juice and vinegar, stirring until blended. (Dressing should be thick.) Makes about 6 cups.

CUCUMBER DRESSING

2 medium cucumbers
2 small onions
4 tablespoons sugar
3 tablespoons lemon juice

4 teaspoons Worcestershire
Dash of garlic powder
2⅔ cups mayonnaise or salad dressing

Grate cucumber and onion; then drain well. Pat dry with paper towels.

Combine remaining ingredients; stir until blended. Add cucumber and onion, stirring well. Makes about 5⅓ cups.

GUACAMOLE

2 small avocados, peeled and mashed
1 tablespoon lemon juice
1 medium onion, minced
1 small clove garlic, crushed
1 large tomato, peeled and finely chopped

½ teaspoon salt
½ teaspoon seasoned salt
½ teaspoon seasoned pepper
½ teaspoon chili powder
Dash of hot sauce

Combine all ingredients; mix well. Cover and chill thoroughly. Serve over salad greens. Makes about 2 cups. Note: May be served as a dip with corn chips.

FRUITY FROZEN SALAD

16 oz. Cool Whip
2 cups sour cream
2 tablespoons lemon juice
1¼ cups sugar

12 bananas, mashed
2 cups crushed pineapple, drained
⅔ cup maraschino cherries
1 cup pecans

Mix first four ingredients together. Add the last four ingredients. Put into a shallow steam table pan, and freeze. Remove from freezer 10-15 minutes before serving. Makes 32 servings.

MILLIONAIRE SALAD

6 eggs
1 cup + 1½ teaspoons sugar
⅓ cup lemon juice
20 oz. whipped cream (3¼ cups after whipping)

½ #10 can white cherries, halved
½ #10 can pineapple tidbits
½ #10 can mandarin sections or fruit cocktail
1¼ pound tiny marshmallows

Drain all fruit well. Combine eggs, sugar, and lemon juice. Cook in double boiler, stirring until thick and smooth. Cool. Add whipped cream. Fold in remaining ingredients. Refrigerate 12 hours. Makes 31 servings.

GRAPEFRUIT FRENCH DRESSING

1⅓ cups vegetable oil
½ cup vinegar
½ cup fresh grapefruit juice
2 teaspoons salt

2 teaspoons sugar
2 teaspoons paprika
2 teaspoons dried tarragon leaves or dried parsley flakes

Combine all ingredients, mixing well; cover and refrigerate 1 to 2 hours. Makes 2½ cups.

ORANGE CARROT SALAD

2 6-oz. packages orange-flavored gelatin
4 cups boiling water
3 cups cold water
4 large carrots, shredded
2 11-oz. cans mandarin oranges, drained

2 15½-oz. cans crushed pineapple,
  undrained
1 cup chopped pecans
Lettuce
Carrot curls
Pecan halves

Dissolve gelatin in boiling water, and stir in cold water. Chill until partially set.

Fold carrots, oranges, pineapple, and chopped pecans into thickened gelatin. Spoon into an oiled 4-quart mold; chill until set. Unmold on lettuce, and garnish with carrot curls and pecan halves. Makes 24-30 servings.

PECAN-STUFFED EGGS

24 hard-cooked eggs
1 cup mayonnaise
2 cups chopped pecans
4 teaspoons grated onion

4 teaspoons vinegar
2 teaspoons dry mustard
2 teaspoons salt
2 teaspoons minced parsley

Slice eggs in half lengthwise, and carefully remove yolks. Mash yolks with a fork; add next 7 ingredients, mixing well. Spoon pecan mixture into egg whites. Garnish with parsley sprigs, if desired. Makes 24 servings.

CUCUMBERS IN SOUR CREAM

12 large cucumbers, peeled and thinly sliced
4 tablespoons salt
8 tablespoons vinegar

4 8-oz. cartons commercial sour
  cream
2 teaspoons chopped fresh chives
2 teaspoons pepper

Place cucumbers in a medium bowl; sprinkle with salt, and let stand 1 hour. Drain cucumbers on paper towels, pressing to remove excess liquid. Return to bowl; stir in remaining ingredients. Chill at least 1 hour. Makes 24-32 servings.

FRESH VEGETABLE MARINATE

8 stalks fresh broccoli
16 large fresh mushrooms, sliced
2 medium-sized green peppers, chopped
6 stalks celery, chopped
2 small heads cauliflower, broken into
  flowerets
2 cups sugar

4 teaspoons dry mustard
2 teaspoons salt
1 cup vinegar
3 cups vegetable oil
2 small onions, grated
4 tablespoons poppy seeds

Remove flowerets from broccoli; cut into bite-sized pieces. Reserve stalks for other use. Combine flowerets, mushrooms, pepper, celery, and cauliflower; toss lightly.

Combine remaining ingredients; mix well, and pour over vegetables. Chill at least 3 hours. Makes 20-24 servings.

SAUERKRAUT SALAD

6 cups chopped sauerkraut, drained
1½ cups sugar
1½ cups thinly sliced celery
1½ green peppers, cut into thin strips

1½ cups grated carrots
1½ chopped onions
3 2-oz. jars chopped pimiento,
    drained

Combine sauerkraut and sugar, mixing well; let stand 30 minutes. Add remaining ingredients; stir well. Cover and chill at least 12 hours. Makes 24 servings.

CHILLED BEAN SALAD

3 10-oz. packages frozen sliced green beans
3 10-oz. packages frozen lima beans
3 10-oz. packages frozen English peas
1½ cups chopped onion
6 hard-cooked eggs, chopped

3 8-oz. cans water chestnuts, drained
    and chopped
1½ cups mayonnaise
3 teaspoons prepared mustard
¾ teaspoon salt

Cook beans and peas according to package directions; drain and let cool. Add onion, eggs, and water chestnuts. Combine mayonnaise, mustard, and salt, mixing well; stir into bean mixture. Cover and chill 8 hours or overnight. Makes 18-24 servings.

CARROT SALAD

4 pounds carrots, sliced diagonally
4 cups chopped celery
2 cups chopped green pepper
4 medium onions, thinly sliced
4 teaspoons celery seeds

4 cups sugar
2 cups vinegar
2 cups water
1⅓ cups vegetable oil

Cook carrots in boiling salted water about 10 minutes or until crisp-tender; drain well.

Place carrots, celery, green pepper, onion, and celery seeds in a large shallow dish; toss lightly, and set aside.

Combine remaining ingredients in a small saucepan, mixing well; bring to a boil, stirring often. Pour over vegetables; cover and chill 8 to 10 hours or overnight. Makes 24 servings.

Main Dishes

AVIS' KING RANCH CHICKEN

1 hen, boiled until tender
1 dozen tortillas

1 large onion, chopped fine
2 cups grated cheese

Sauce:
Blend 1 can cream of mushroom soup, 1 can cream chicken soup, ½ can tomatoes with green chilies, ½ can chicken broth. Bone chicken and cut into small pieces. Grease casserole. Make a layer of chicken, a layer of tortillas torn in small pieces, and a layer of grated cheese. Sprinkle onion over cheese, and pour sauce over mixture. Then repeat, starting with chicken. Bake at 350° for 1 hour, uncovered. Serves 10.

SWISS STEAK

1½ pounds round steak, cut 1-inch thick
½ cup flour
1 tablespoon dry mustard
2 tablespoons oil
Salt and pepper to taste
1 1-pound can tomatoes

1 tablespoon lemon juice
1 large onion, chopped
½ cup celery, diced
3 carrots, diced
2 tablespoons Worcestershire
1 tablespoon brown sugar

Mix flour, mustard, salt, and pepper. Sprinkle mixture over meat and pound with a meat pounder. Cut into individual portions and brown lightly in oil. Put meat in a casserole and add remaining ingredients. Cover and bake for 2½ hours at 300°. (Test with a fork at two hours; if meat is tender, remove from oven then to avoid overcooking.) Serves 6.

PEPPER STEAK

1½ pounds round steak
½ cup tomato catsup
1½ tablespoons flour
2 bouillon cubes
2 tablespoons soy sauce

1½ cups water
Salt and pepper to taste
1 medium onion, sliced
1 4-oz. can mushroom pieces
2 green peppers, sliced

Cut steak in serving size strips. Brown lightly in hot skillet in small amount of oil. Remove meat. Mix catsup, flour, bouillon, soy sauce, and water; pour into skillet. Simmer for 5 minutes. Return meat to skillet. Cover and cook over low heat until steak is tender—about 1½ hours. Add salt and pepper, onions, mushrooms, and peppers. Cover and continue to cook over low heat until vegetables are tender. Serve with rice or mashed potatoes. Serves 5.

PEANUT BUTTER CHICKEN

1 2½ to 3-pound broiler-fryer chicken, cut into
   pieces
¼ cup flour
1 egg
⅓ cup peanut butter

1 teaspoon salt
⅛ teaspoon pepper
⅓ cup milk
½ cup dry bread crumbs
¼ cup oil

Wash and dry chicken pieces. Dip in flour. Blend egg, peanut butter, salt, and pepper. Gradually add milk, beating with fork to blend. Dip floured chicken in peanut butter mixture and then in crumbs. Place on oiled baking dish. Drizzle remaining oil over chicken and bake for 45 minutes at 375°. (Test for tenderness; bake longer if needed.)

OVEN-BARBECUED CHICKEN

2 1½-pound broiling chickens, cut into pieces
2 teaspoons salt substitute
4 teaspoons Worcestershire
2 bay leaves
½ cup lemon juice
1 cup water

1 cup tomato juice
½ teaspoon dry mustard
2 cloves garlic, finely chopped
½ teaspoon paprika
¼ teaspoon cayenne pepper
1 teaspoon sugar or sugar substitute

Wash and dry chicken. Mix other ingredients in a saucepan and cook for 10 minutes. Place chickens on broiling rack and spoon sauce over it. Broil for 10 minutes. Turn and baste with sauce, continuing to cook for about 45 minutes, or until chicken is tender.

BARBECUED RED SNAPPER

Follow instructions for Oven Barbecued Chicken.

HOT CHICKEN SALAD PINWHEEL

6 cups diced cooked chicken
1 cup chopped celery
1 cup chopped green pepper
1 cup chopped onion
2 cups frozen English peas, thawed
Salt and pepper to taste
1⅓ cups mayonnaise

4 8-oz. cans crescent dinner rolls
1 cup shredded sharp cheddar cheese
16 slices cooked bacon, crumbled, or
   1 cup imitation bacon
4 eggs, beaten
4 10½ oz. cans asparagus tips, drained
   (optional)

Combine first 7 ingredients; mix well and set aside. Separate crescent rolls into triangles. Arrange 4 triangles on a greased baking sheet with the points outward and the bases forming a square in the center of the pan.

Arrange remaining 4 triangles over the first 4 triangles with the point outward and the bases forming a second square at a 45° turn over the first square. Press overlapping part of triangles slightly to mesh bases and form a 2-inch circle in the center of the pan. Do the same with the remaining triangles.

Spoon chicken mixture onto crescent pinwheel, forming a ring. Sprinkle with cheese and bacon. Bring points of triangles over the chicken mixture, and secure tips under the edges of the circle, stretching triangles slightly as necessary. Brush with beaten egg. Bake at 350° for 25 minutes or until crust is golden brown; place on a warm serving platter. Makes 16-24 servings.

If desired, heat the asparagus tips, and arrange in center of pinwheel.

ANNE'S EGG CASSEROLE

6 hard-cooked eggs
2 teaspoons dry mustard
2 tablespoons sour cream
Italian dressing
Dash salt

Mash egg yolks and mix with other ingredients; then return to halved whites.

2 tablespoons butter
1 medium green pepper, chopped
⅓ cup chopped onion

Sauté the above in a small amount of oil. Then add two tablespoons chopped pimiento, 8 ounces sour cream, and 1 can cream of mushroom soup, undiluted. Mix well; then pour into a casserole. Place eggs in the sauce and grate ½ cup cheddar cheese over the top. Place in 350° oven until sauce bubbles. Serve in chafing dish—or in the casserole dish in which it was cooked. Serves 4-6.

WINTER CASSEROLE

1½ pounds pork sausage, cut in 14 patties
½ cup chopped onion
½ cup chopped green pepper
3 cups chopped fresh tomatoes or canned
  tomatoes, drained
6-ounce can tomato paste
½ teaspoon salt

⅛ teaspoon pepper
½ teaspoon basil
½ teaspoon oregano
½ cup Parmesan cheese
12-oz. package corn muffin mix
1 cup grated cheddar cheese

Lightly brown sausage patties in skillet and drain on paper towel. Drain off all but 2 tablespoons fat from skillet. Add onion and green pepper; cook until tender but not brown. Add next six ingredients and simmer five minutes.

Mix Parmesan and corn muffin mix; then prepare cornbread as directed on package. Spread in greased shallow 2-quart baking dish. Arrange half of the sausage patties on cornbread mixture, cover with tomato mixture, and arrange remaining patties on top. Bake 20 minutes. Sprinkle with cheese and bake 10 minutes longer. 6 to 8 servings.

VEAL IN CREAM SAUCE

4 pounds lean veal stew meat
2 teaspoons sugar
½ cup thinly sliced onion
3 cups chicken broth
1 tablespoon butter
1 tablespoon flour

1 cup half-and-half
Salt and pepper to taste
1 teaspoon grated lemon peel
1 tablespoon slivered lemon peel
Chopped parsley

Cook sugar and onion in a heavy skillet over low heat until onions are glazed and soft. Add veal and chicken broth. Cover and simmer until the veal is tender (about 1 hour). Mix the butter and flour together and blend with some of the liquid; then add the remainder. Cook until thickened. Add half-and-half, seasonings, and grated lemon peel. Turn off the heat and let stand for at least one hour. Then reheat and serve with the slivered lemon peel and parsley sprinkled on top. Serve with brown rice.

EGGPLANT CASSEROLE

3 large eggplants
1½ cups salt
9 quarts water
6 eggs, well beaten
6 tablespoons milk
4½ cups bacon-flavored cracker crumbs
1½ cups margarine, melted
3 pounds ground chuck
3 large onions, chopped
3 large green peppers, chopped

3 teaspoons seasoned salt
1½ teaspoons pepper
3 teaspoons dried whole oregano
3 bay leaves, crumbled
6 medium tomatoes, cut into ½-inch
  slices
3 cups shredded extra sharp cheddar
  cheese, divided
1½ cups grated Parmesan cheese
6 eggs, well beaten
1½ cups milk

Peel eggplant, and cut into ½-inch slices. Dissolve 1½ cup salt in water; add eggplant, and soak for 30 minutes. Drain well, and pat dry.

Combine 6 eggs and 6 tablespoons milk, mixing well. Dip eggplant in mixture, and coat with cracker crumbs. Fry a few at a time in 1½ cups margarine, just until browned, turning once. Repeat until all are browned; drain on paper towels.

Sauté ground chuck with chopped onion and green pepper until beef is lightly browned. Stir in seasoned salt, pepper, oregano, and bay leaves.

Layer one-third of eggplant, half each of beef mixture, tomato slices, and cheddar cheese in a greased steam table pan. Repeat layers. Place remaining eggplant on top, and sprinkle with Parmesan cheese.

Combine 6 eggs and 1½ cup milk, mixing well; pour over casserole. Bake at 375° for 35 minutes. Makes 24 servings.

IRENE'S MUSHROOM MACARONI AND CHEESE

3 cups cooked macaroni
1 tablespoon butter or margarine
1 10½-oz. can condensed cream of mushroom soup

⅓ cup water
2 cups shredded cheddar cheese
1 tablespoon finely minced onion

Blend hot cooked macaroni with butter in 1½-quart casserole. Stir in soup, water, 1½ cups cheese, and onion. Sprinkle remaining cheese on top. Bake in a 350° oven about 30 minutes or until brown and bubbly. 4 servings.

BAKED PORK CHOPS

6 to 8 pork chops
1 can cream of mushroom soup

1 can beef bouillon

Brown chops in skillet. Mix bouillon and mushroom soup together and pour over chops. Bake, uncovered, at 350° for one hour.

Serve with rice.

CASHEW TUNA CASSEROLE

1 3-oz. can chow mein noodles
1 can condensed cream of mushroom soup
¼ cup water
1 7-oz. can chunk-style tuna
¼ pound cashew nuts
1 cup finely diced celery

1 tablespoon chopped green pepper
¼ cup minced onion
⅛ teaspoon salt (omit if cashews are
    salted)
⅛ teaspoon pepper

Combine all ingredients except ½ cup noodles in a casserole. Sprinkle reserved noodles on top. Bake, uncovered, at 325° for 40 minutes. Makes 5 servings.

CHICKEN AND SWEET CREAM BISCUITS

10-12 chicken breasts
2 teaspoons salt
1 cup chopped celery
⅓ cup chopped onion
5 carrots, sliced crosswise
¼ cup chicken fat

2 cups chicken broth
¾ cup flour
2 cups light cream
2 egg yolks, beaten
Parsley
Sweet Cream Biscuits (see p. 85)

Place chicken breasts in kettle. Add hot water to cover. Add salt, celery and onion, and simmer, covered, until tender—about 3 hours. Add carrots the last 30 minutes of cooking. Drain broth from chicken. Skim fat from broth, saving ¼ cup fat for gravy. Strain broth; save carrots. Measure 2 cups broth for gravy. Pour remaining broth back into kettle with chicken to keep hot. Measure chicken fat into saucepan; blend in flour. Gradually add broth and cream. Cook until thick and smooth, stirring constantly. Add a small amount of hot gravy to egg yolks; then add yolks to gravy. Cook 2 minutes more. Place hot chicken and carrots in serving dish and pour in gravy. Sprinkle with parsley and top with baked sweet cream biscuits. Makes 10 to 12 servings.

TEX-MEX EGGS

1 tablespoon margarine
1 small onion, minced
1 clove garlic, crushed
1 4-oz. can green chilies

1 16-oz. can tomatoes, chopped
¼ pound Jalapeno cheese, diced
4 eggs

Heat margarine; sauté onion and garlic until transparent. Add tomatoes and cook until fairly dry. Place in oven-proof dish. Add cheese and place in oven until almost melted.

Break 4 eggs into dish and bake at 350° until eggs are set (about 12 minutes). Serve with toasted garlic bread or hot tortillas. Serves 2.

COMPANY SCRAMBLED EGGS

6 eggs
½ cup grated cheddar cheese

Salt and pepper to taste
½ stick butter or margarine

In blender, whip eggs and cheese at highest speed. Add salt and pepper. Melt butter in top of double boiler. Pour in egg and cheese mixture and stir until done. Serves 3-4.

CHICKEN QUICHE

1 pie shell, baked and cooled
1 cup cooked chicken, finely chopped
1 cup grated Swiss cheese
¼ cup chopped onion
1 tablespoon flour

2 eggs, well beaten
½ teaspoon mustard (powder)
1 cup milk
½ cup pecans, chopped

Mix chicken, Swiss cheese, onion, and flour. Add pecans. Pour into baked crust. Mix eggs, milk, and mustard and pour over chicken mixture. Bake at 325° for about fifty minutes. Makes 5 or 6 servings.

BEEF STROGANOFF

2 pounds round steak
1 stick butter
4 medium onions, chopped
1 8-oz. can tomato paste

½ cup water
1 8-oz. can mushrooms
2 cups sour cream
Salt and pepper to taste

Cut beef in long, thin strips. Melt butter in a skillet and brown the meat. Season with salt and pepper. Add chopped onions, tomato paste, and water. Simmer for 1½ hours, or until meat is tender. About 30 minutes before serving, add mushrooms and sour cream. Heat slowly; high temperature will curdle the cream. Serve on top of cooked noodles. Serves 10.

COMPANY HOT DOGS

2 tablespoons butter
1-pound package wieners, cut in ½-inch slices
10¾-oz. can condensed cream of celery soup
8-oz. package frozen mixed vegetables with onion
    sauce, thawed

1 cup milk
¼ teaspoon marjoram leaves
10-oz. can refrigerated big flaky biscuits
⅔ cup shredded cheddar cheese

Preheat oven to 375°. In 10-inch ovenproof fry pan, brown butter and wieners. Stir in soup, mixed vegetables, milk, and marjoram; heat until hot and bubbly. Separate biscuit dough into 10 biscuits; cut each into 4 pieces. Arrange over hot wiener mixture with points up. Bake 20 to 25 minutes until biscuits are golden brown. Remove from oven; sprinkle with cheese. Serve immediately. 5 servings.

GRAPEFRUIT CHICKEN CASSEROLE

3 tablespoons butter
1 cup sliced fresh mushrooms
2 tablespoons chopped onion
5 tablespoons flour
¾ cup chicken stock
¾ cup milk
¾ teaspoon salt

Pepper to taste
2 eggs, slightly beaten
1½ cups diced cooked chicken
¾ cup diced cooked ham
1 cup grapefruit sections, cut in pieces
¼ cup sliced stuffed olives
½ cup grated Parmesan cheese

Melt butter in 3-quart casserole and brown mushrooms and onions in it. Blend in flour. Gradually add stock and milk and cook over low heat, stirring constantly, until thickened. Add salt and pepper. Combine mixture with eggs and cook 2 minutes longer, stirring constantly. Remove from heat and add chicken, ham, grapefruit sections, and olives. Mix well. Sprinkle top with cheese and bake in 350° until brown on top (20-25 minutes). Serves 4.

WILD RICE AND CHICKEN LIVERS

1 cup wild rice
1 pound chicken livers
¼ cup butter
1 medium onion, chopped
1 clove garlic, mashed

Salt and pepper to taste
2 tablespoons flour
1½ cups heavy cream
¼ cup water

Wash rice thoroughly in cold water. Cook in 6 cups boiling salted water until tender (30-40 minutes). Drain and place in a 2½-3-quart casserole. Sauté chicken livers in butter until nicely browned. Add onion and garlic and brown lightly. Season. Sprinkle flour over and stir to mix well. Add to rice in casserole. Pour in cream and water. Bake in 375° oven 20 minutes. Serves 4.

LINDA'S EGGS A LA KING IN A
SAUSAGE RING

Eggs a la King
2 cups well seasoned white sauce
8 hard-cooked eggs, cut in quarters
8 oz. sliced mushrooms
4 tablespoons chopped green pepper
4 tablespoons chopped pimiento

Sausage Ring
2 pounds bulk sausage
2 eggs, beaten
2 tablespoons grated onion
1½ cups fine dry bread crumbs
¼ cup chopped parsley

Fold ingredients for Eggs a la King into white sauce.

Mix ingredients well and pack into a lightly buttered 9-inch ring mold. Bake at 350° for 20 minutes. Take from oven and pour off excess fat. Bake 20 minutes longer. Turn onto heated platter and fill with Eggs a la King.

(When baking the sausage ring, you may want to put the mold in a larger pan to catch the spillover.)

GOLDENROD EGGS

Make Eggs a la King. Boil six eggs, reserving yolk. Serve Eggs a la King on buttered whole wheat toast, English muffins, or biscuits. Put egg yolks through sieve and sprinkle over Eggs a la King.

MARY B'S WESTERN OMELETTE

¾ pound bacon, diced
1½ pound onions, diced
1½ pound green peppers, diced
¾ pound ham trimmings
90 eggs, medium to large size

1 pt. milk
½ oz. salt
¼ teaspoon pepper, white
Butter as needed

Dice bacon, onions, and green peppers into ¼-inch pieces. Fry diced bacon in frying pan. Add onions and green peppers; sauté until onions are transparent, but not brown. Add diced ham and heat thoroughly. Remove from heat. Break eggs into bowl, being careful that shell particles don't fall into eggs. Add milk, salt, and white pepper, and beat well. Heat butter in frying pan and pour off excess fat. Add western mixture, allowing 1 oz. per serving and egg mixture, equivalent to two eggs per serving. Cook over hot fire, continuously moving frying pan back and forth until eggs become firm, but are still soft in the middle. Use spatula and fold eggs in from bottom of frying pan toward the opposite rim from handle to form a pointed oval. Allow to brown lightly, and turn over on plate or pan. Makes 50 servings.

RUBY LEE'S CHICKEN CASSEROLE

2½ cups Uncle Ben's uncooked rice
½ large can mushroom soup
½ large can water
⅓ cup onion soup mix

1 tablespoon sugar
¾ cup soy sauce
20 chicken breasts, split
Salt and pepper to taste

Allow 1¼ cups uncooked rice for each shallow steam table pan. Mix all other ingredients except chicken. Pour this over rice and stir to mix. Place chicken on top of rice. Pat down gently to get some of the sauce on top of chicken. Make sure rice stays on the bottom. Cover with foil and cook about 2 hours at 350°. Makes 20 servings.

SALMON CROQUETTES

1½ #4 can salmon
2½ quarts potatoes, mashed
⅛ cup Worcestershire sauce

17 eggs
1½ onions
Cracker crumbs

Mix and chill the salmon, potatoes, Worcestershire sauce, eggs, and salt. Make into cone-shaped croquettes and roll in cracker crumbs. Fry in deep fat. Makes 30 servings.

FRUITED HAM

A slice of ham, about 1 inch thick, in a casserole.

Cover the ham slice with sliced pineapple, apricots, and apples (canned). Sprinkle with cinnamon and cloves. Cover. Place in 325° oven for 45 minutes, basting several times with juices from fruits.

SALMON LOAF

2 cups canned salmon
1½ cups cooked mashed potatoes
¼ pound grated cheese
¼ teaspoon salt
⅛ teaspoon paprika

Dash cayenne pepper (optional)
2 tablespoons butter
1½ to 2 tablespoons flour
1 cup milk

Melt butter in heavy skillet. Stir in flour, mixing well. Add milk and stir until smooth—over low heat. Add cheese, salt, pepper. Grease a casserole and place mashed potatoes in the bottom. Cover them with half the cheese sauce. Flake salmon and place over sauce; then cover with remaining sauce. Bake at 300° for about 30 minutes.

CREAMED EGGS AND HAM—DANISH

3 pounds cooked ham
¼ pound green bell peppers
2 oz. pimiento
2 oz. butter

1½ quarts cream sauce
25 whole fresh eggs
25 English muffins

Cook eggs sunny-side up. Dice and simmer cooked ham, green peppers, pimiento, and butter for 10 minutes. Add cream sauce. Assemble English muffin and cooked eggs, and pour creamed mixture over all when ready to serve. Makes 25 servings.

VEAL PARMESAN

12 (6 oz. each) breaded veal cutlets
1 cup finely chopped onion
½ teaspoon ground thyme
½ cup butter or margarine

1 can (50 oz.) tomato sauce
12 slices Mozzarella cheese
¾ cup grated Parmesan cheese

Prepare cutlets to package directions. Drain; arrange in baking pan (12 × 20 × 2″). Cook onion with thyme in butter until tender. Add tomato sauce; pour over veal. Top each slice veal with Mozzarella and Parmesan cheese. Bake at 350° for 40 minutes or until hot. Makes 12 servings.

PINEAPPLE CHICKEN AND RICE

100 pieces fresh chicken
Flour, salt, pepper as needed
1¾ gallon pineapple juice

3 cups lemon juice
3 cups soy sauce
2½ #10 can sliced pineapple

Toss chicken lightly in flour; season with salt and pepper. Brown each piece in deep fat. Place chicken in roasting or serving pans. Pour the liquid mixture over all and cover. Bake at 350° for 40 to 45 minutes. Sauté pineapple slices easy, one slice per serving. Place sautéed pineapple over chicken. Return to oven for 15 minutes. Serve with steamed white rice. Makes 100 servings.

RAISIN HAM

1 #10 can pineapple chunks
16 cups diced cooked ham
2½ cups golden raisins
5 medium onions, thinly sliced and separated into
    rings
5 small green peppers, sliced into rings
⅓ cup vinegar

2 tablespoons dry mustard
2½ cups firmly packed brown sugar
¼ cup cornstarch
1 teaspoon salt
5 tablespoons soy sauce
5 tablespoons Worcestershire sauce
Hot cooked rice

Drain pineapple, reserving liquid; add enough water to liquid to measure 5 cups. Set pineapple and liquid aside.

Place ham in a lightly greased steam table pan; sprinkle raisins over ham. Layer onion, green pepper, and pineapple over ham and raisins.

Combine reserved pineapple liquid, vinegar, mustard, sugar, cornstarch, and salt in a small saucepan, stirring until cornstarch is dissolved. Cook mixture over low heat, stirring constantly, until thickened. Stir in soy sauce and Worcestershire sauce; pour over ham and vegetables. Bake at 350° for 45 minutes. Serve over hot cooked rice. Makes 30 servings.

CHICKEN MARENGO

9-10 pounds fresh chicken, quartered
¾ cup sliced fresh mushrooms
2 tablespoons butter or margarine

1¼ cups brown gravy
2½ cups tomato sauce

In a baking pan (12 × 20 × 2″), place chicken skin side up. Sprinkle with salt and pepper. Bake uncovered at 400° for 30 minutes. Drain off excess fat. Cook mushrooms in butter until tender. Stir in sauces. Bring to a boil; pour over the chicken. Bake 40 minutes or until done. Remove chicken. Thicken sauce if desired. Makes 16 servings (¼ chicken each).

CHICKEN PARMIGIANA

12 whole chicken breasts, split, boned, and skinned
8 eggs, slightly beaten
4 teaspoons salt
2 teaspoons pepper
3 cups fine, dry bread crumbs
2 cups vegetable oil
4 15-oz. cans tomato sauce

1 teaspoon dried whole basil
½ teaspoon garlic powder
4 tablespoons butter or margarine
2 cups grated Parmesan cheese
2 pounds Mozzarella cheese, thinly sliced
    and cut into triangles

Place each chicken breast on a sheet of waxed paper. Flatten to ¼-inch thickness, using a meat mallet or rolling pin. Combine eggs, salt, and pepper. Dip chicken breasts into egg mixture and roll each in bread crumbs. Brown chicken in hot oil in a large skillet; drain on paper towels. Place chicken in a lightly greased shallow steam table baking pan.

Drain oil from skillet. Combine tomato sauce, basil, and garlic powder in skillet. Bring to a boil, and simmer 10 minutes or until thickened. Stir in butter. Pour mixture over chicken, and sprinkle with Parmesan cheese.

Cover and bake at 350° for 30 minutes. Uncover and arrange mozzarella cheese slices on top. Bake 10 additional minutes. Makes 24 servings.

WHITE FISH IN CHEESE SAUCE

8 pounds frozen white fish fillets, thawed
1 50 oz. can cheese sauce
½ cup chopped onion

½ cup chopped parsley
¼ cup lemon juice

Dry fish fillets on absorbent paper. Blend sauce, onion, and parsley. Spread half of sauce over bottom of 2 baking pans (12 × 20 × 2"). Arrange fillets over sauce; sprinkle with lemon juice. Cover with remaining sauce. Bake at 400° for 30 minutes or until done. Stir sauce before serving. Makes 32 servings of 4 ounces each.

MARY ALICE'S CHICKEN ENCHILADA CASSEROLE

1 fryer (boiled and boned)
1 can cream of celery soup
1 can cream of mushroom soup
1 medium onion, chopped
½ can Rotel (a whole can makes it hotter)

1 green bell pepper, chopped
1½ cups chicken broth
Salt and pepper
1 package frozen tortillas

Mix everything together except tortillas. Alternate layers of tortillas torn in ¼ pieces with chicken mixture. Bake 30 or 40 minutes at 350°. Sprinkle with grated cheese and bake 5 minutes longer.

CORNBREAD TOPPING (use with Hot Tamale Pie)

1 pound all-purpose flour
¾ cup sugar
1 tablespoon salt
4½ teaspoon baking powder

2 pounds yellow corn meal
2 cups salad oil
8 eggs, beaten
1¼ quarts milk

Sift dry ingredients. Add salad oil, eggs, and milk, and mix well. Pour over meat and vegetable mix.

HOT TAMALE PIE

8 pounds ground beef	½ pound pimientos or red peppers, fine
½ clove garlic	2½-pound package whole kernel corn
2 pounds onion, finely chopped	2½ quarts tomatoes, whole
1 pound green peppers, finely chopped	½ quart tomato paste
1½ pound celery, diced small	2 cups bacon fat

Sauté meat in bacon fat until brown. Cook garlic, onion, green pepper, and celery in fat until vegetables are tender but not brown. Combine tomatoes and tomato paste; mix well and add to vegetables and meat. Add corn and pimiento to meat mixture; thoroughly mix. Pour mixture into steam table pans and pour over cornbread topping. Bake in hot oven 375° for 40-45 minutes. Makes 50 servings of 6 ounces each.

ZUCCHINI-BEEF CASSEROLE

5 pounds ground beef	5 pounds zucchini, sliced ½" round
½ can tomato catsup (add ⅛ #10 can water)	2½ tablespoons butter or margarine (for greasing casserole)
5 teaspoons salt	1 5-pound loaf, cream cheese, softened
1¼ teaspoons Tabasco	½ tub sour cream
5 teaspoons Worcestershire	½ teaspoon paprika
2½ onions, chopped	2 cups croutons

Brown beef. Add tomato sauce, salt, Tabasco, Worcestershire, and cook about 5 minutes. Add green onions. Remove from heat. In steam table pan, place a layer of meat mixture and a layer of zucchini, repeat. Blend cream cheese and sour cream. Spread over top of casserole and sprinkle with paprika. Cover with croutons or Parmesan cheese. Bake in 300° oven for 35 minutes. Serve hot. Makes 4 steam table pans.

PORK CHOPS ITALIANO

24 1-inch-thick loin pork chops	12 medium-size green peppers, cut into thin strips
Salt and pepper to taste	1 5-oz. can tomato sauce
¼ cup vegetable oil	1½ teaspoon whole oregano or basil
3 pounds fresh mushrooms, sliced	¼ cup lemon juice
6 medium onions, chopped	
5 small clove garlic, crushed	

Sprinkle pork chops with salt and pepper; brown on both sides in hot oil. Place chops in a shallow steam table pan; cover with mushrooms, and set aside.

Add onion, garlic, and green pepper to skillet; cook until tender. Add remaining ingredients, and simmer 5 minutes; pour over chops. Bake at 350° for 1 hour or until chops are done. Makes 24 servings.

SAUSAGE CASSEROLE

2 pounds mild bulk pork sausage	1¼ cups milk
1 teaspoon prepared mustard	¾ cup half-and-half
12 slices thin-sliced sandwich bread, crusts removed	¼ teaspoon Worcestershire sauce
6 sandwich-size slices Swiss cheese	Dash of pepper
3 eggs	Dash of ground nutmeg

Cook sausage until browned, stirring to crumble; drain well. Combine sausage and mustard, stirring until blended. Cut bread slices in half diagonally. Space half of bread evenly in a greased 12 × 8 × 2-inch baking dish. Sprinkle sausage over bread; top with cheese slices. Space remaining bread halves evenly on top of cheese slices.

Combine remaining ingredients; beat until blended. Pour egg mixture over bread in baking dish. Cover and refrigerate overnight.

Bake, uncovered, at 350° for 35 to 40 minutes or until egg mixture is set. Makes 8 to 10 servings.

HOT SEAFOOD PIE

10 cups crushed potato chips, divided
2 cups melted margarine
8 6½-oz. cans crabmeat, drained and flaked
8 4½-oz. cans medium shrimp, drained
4 cups chopped celery
2 cups chopped green pepper

4 tablespoons grated onion
8 tablespoons lemon juice
1 teaspoon salt
1 cup chopped pimiento
4 cups mayonnaise
2 cups shredded cheddar cheese

Combine 6 cups crushed potato chips and margarine; press into a 9-inch pieplate. Bake at 375° for 5 minutes. Cool.

Combine crabmeat, shrimp, celery, green pepper, onion, lemon juice, salt, pimiento, and mayonnaise in a large bowl; stir well. Spoon mixture into potato chip crust. Combine remaining crushed potato chips and cheese; sprinkle on top. Bake at 375° for 10 minutes or until cheese melts. Makes 24-32 servings.

MARINATED PORK ROAST

4 tablespoons dry mustard
4 teaspoons whole thyme leaves
1 cup soy sauce
4 cloves garlic, minced
2 teaspoons ground ginger

1 8-10-pound pork loin roast, boned,
    rolled, and tied
2 10-oz. jars apricot preserves or jelly
2 tablespoons soy sauce

Combine first 5 ingredients in a shallow dish, stirring well. Place roast in dish; cover and marinate 3 to 4 hours in refrigerator, turning occasionally.

Remove roast from marinade, and place on a rack in a shallow roasting pan. Insert meat thermometer at an angle into thickest part of roast. Bake, uncovered, at 325° until thermometer registers 170° (2½ to 3 hours total cooking time).

Combine preserves and 2 tablespoons soy sauce in a small saucepan; cook over low heat, stirring occasionally, until preserves melt. Serve with sliced roast. Garnish as desired. Makes 24-28 servings.

ROUND STEAK DE PARMESAN

7 pounds boneless round steak, ¾ inch thick
5 eggs, beaten
1⅔ cups milk
2⅓ cups fine dry bread crumbs
2 tablespoons salt
¾ teaspoon pepper
5 tablespoons Accent

1 cup bacon drippings
2⅓ cups water
1¼ teaspoons dried whole oregano
1¼ teaspoons grated Parmesan cheese
1 #10 can small onions
1¼ teaspoons salt
1¼ teaspoons paprika

Trim excess fat from steak; pound to ½-inch thickness. Cut steak into serving-size pieces.

Combine egg and milk; beat well. Combine bread crumbs, 2 tablespoons salt, pepper, and Accent. Dip steak in egg mixture, dredge in bread crumb mixture, and brown in bacon drippings. Place steak in lightly greased steam table pan. Add water and sprinkle with oregano and cheese.

Add onions to steak; sprinkle with 1¼ teaspoon salt and paprika. Cover tightly and bake at 325° for 1 hour and 15 minutes or until tender. Makes 30 servings.

SAUSAGE AND BROCCOLI CASSEROLE

4 pounds sausage links, cut into small pieces
4 10-oz. packages frozen chopped broccoli
1 cup shredded mild cheddar cheese
12 tablespoons chopped green pepper
12 tablespoons minced fresh parsley
8 tablespoons grated onion
8 tablespoons all-purpose flour
12 hard-cooked eggs, sliced

4 10¾-oz. cans cream of mushroom soup, diluted
1⅓ cups milk
2 cups dry bread crumbs
12 tablespoons melted butter or margarine
Hot cooked rice

Cook sausage until browned; drain. Cook broccoli according to package directions; drain well. Place broccoli in a lightly greased steam table pan.

Combine sausage, cheese, green pepper, onion, parsley, and flour in a medium bowl; spoon half of sausage mixture over broccoli in casserole. Top sausage mixture with egg slices; spoon remaining sausage mixture over eggs.

Combine soup and milk; pour over casserole. Combine bread crumbs and butter; sprinkle over casserole. Bake at 375° for 30 minutes. Serve over hot cooked rice. Makes 24 servings.

CONNIE'S CREOLE EGGS

10 eggs, hardboiled, cut in medium-sized pieces

Cook together the ingredients below, until tender (may have to add a little water):

1 pint chopped celery
1 can tomatoes
3 pimentos
3 green peppers (chopped)

1 onion
1 teaspoon Worcestershire sauce
1 teaspoon butter
Salt to taste

Sauce:

1 pint sweet milk
⅓ cup butter

3 teaspoons of flour
Salt to taste

Mix together and cook until thick.

Put alternate layers in pan. Bread crumbs and butter may be sprinkled over top. Place in stove to brown.

Vegetables

PEANUTTY SQUASH

2 1-pound cans squash or equivalent amount of
  fresh or frozen squash, cooked
1 2-oz. jar chopped pimiento
2 tablespoons grated onion
8 oz. package herb-seasoned stuffing

2 grated carrots
1 can cream of chicken soup
1 cup sour cream
1 stick margarine, melted
1 cup chopped peanuts

Combine vegetables. Blend undiluted soup and sour cream; stir into vegetable mixture. Toss together stuffing, chopped peanuts, and margarine. Pour half the stuffing in a shallow 3-quart baking dish. Pour vegetable-sour cream mixture over layer. Top with remaining stuffing. Bake at 375° for 30 minutes. Serves 8-10.

ASPARAGUS-PEA CASSEROLE

2 10-oz. packages frozen green peas
1 10½ oz. can cream of mushroom soup
½ cup water

1 2-oz. jar chopped pimiento
1½ cups shredded cheddar cheese
2 10½-oz. cans asparagus tips, drained

Cook peas according to package directions. Drain. Spray casserole with vegetable cooking spray. Combine soup and water. Mix in peas, pimientos, and cheese, reserving enough cheese for topping. Line bottom of casserole with asparagus. Pour soup mixture over asparagus and sprinkle remaining cheese on top. Bake at 350° until bubbly—about 20 minutes. Serves 8.

GREEN BEAN CASSEROLE

3 1-pound cans French-style green beans
1 can cream of celery soup

1 can water chestnuts
8 oz. sharp cheese, grated

Mix together and pour into casserole. Bake for 25 minutes at 350°. Top with 1 can French-fried onion rings.

ONIONS ALMONDINE

1 10½-oz. can cream of celery soup (condensed)
4 cups cooked small white onions, drained

½ cup shredded cheddar cheese
¼ cup chopped toasted almonds

Stir soup until smooth; mix with onions in 1½ quart casserole. Sprinkle cheese and nuts on top. Bake at 375° for 30 minutes. 6 servings.

CHEESE TOMATO CASSEROLE

2 tablespoons chopped onion
2 tablespoons bacon drippings
1 1-pound can tomatoes

1 cup grated sharp cheddar cheese
1 cup crushed potato chips

Cook onion in bacon fat until tender. Add tomatoes. Put layers of tomato mixture, cheese, and potato chips in a casserole, ending with a layer of potato chips. Bake about 20 minutes at 400°. Makes 4 servings.

BAKED SPINACH

2 packages frozen spinach
6 tablespoons butter or margarine
1 8-oz. package cream cheese

2 tablespoons freeze-dried chopped
   chives
½ package herb dressing mix

Cook spinach and drain. Place spinach in greased casserole. Mix two tablespoons margarine with cream cheese and chives, and mix with spinach. Salt and pepper to taste. Sprinkle dressing on top and dot with remaining margarine. Bake at 350° for 30 minutes. Serves 8.

CORN CASSEROLE

1 medium-sized onion, chopped
1 small green pepper, seeded and chopped
2 tablespoons butter or margarine
1 1-pound can cream-style corn
1 12-oz. can white whole-kernel corn

1 4-oz. can chopped pimientos, drained
1 cup sour cream
1 teaspoon cornstarch
1 teaspoon salt
¼ teaspoon black pepper

Sauté onion and green pepper in butter until onion is golden. Add creamed corn, white corn kernels, and chopped pimiento. Blend. Combine sour cream with cornstarch, salt, and pepper. Stir into corn mixture. Pour into a shallow buttered baking dish. Bake for about 20 minutes at 350°. Serves 6.

BROCCOLI SESAME

2 tablespoons sesame seeds, toasted
2 packages frozen chopped broccoli
2 tablespoons oil

2 tablespoons soy sauce
1 tablespoon lemon juice
¼ cup liquid from cooked broccoli

Cook broccoli until about half-done. Drain. Stir-fry in oil for two minutes. Add cooking liquid and soy sauce, cover, and simmer for about five minutes. Add lemon juice and sesame seed.

(To toast sesame seeds, place in heavy skillet over moderate heat. Shake pan continually until they are brown.)

CARROTS AND WHITE GRAPES

1 13½-oz. can small whole carrots
30 seedless white grapes

4 tablespoons butter

Drain carrots and dry with paper towel. Wash and stem grapes and dry. Melt butter over medium heat. Cook grapes and carrots in butter for 4 minutes, stirring constantly. Serve hot.

PEAS IN PATTY SHELLS

¼ cup chopped green onion
1 tablespoon margarine
½ teaspoon sugar or sugar substitute
2 tablespoons flour
½ teaspoon salt
⅛ teaspoon pepper

1 cup half-and-half
1 cup milk
2 teaspoons lemon juice
2 cups cooked frozen peas
1 2-oz. jar chopped pimiento, drained
12 patty shells

Cook onion in margarine until golden. Combine sugar and flour and add to onion mixture. Add salt and pepper and mix. Add half-and-half and milk, and stir over low heat until mixture thickens. Add lemon juice, peas, and pimiento. Serve in patty shells.

SECOND HELPING CARROTS

4 cups sliced peeled carrots
1 medium onion, chopped
3 tablespoons margarine
1 can condensed cream of celery soup
½ teaspoon salt

⅛ teaspoon pepper
½ cup grated sharp cheese
3 cups herb-flavored bread stuffing
⅓ cup melted butter

Cook carrots until tender. Drain. Cook onion in butter until soft. Stir in soup, salt, pepper, cheese, and carrots. Spray 2-quart casserole with vegetable spray and pour carrot mixture in it. Mix stuffing mix with melted butter and spoon over carrots. Bake for about 20 minutes in 350° oven. 6 servings.

SOUR CREAM SPINACH

1 pound frozen spinach, chopped
2 tablespoons chopped onion
1 cup grated Parmesan cheese
1 cup sour cream
2 tablespoons flour

4 tablespoons butter
4 eggs
1 teaspoon salt
½ teaspoon pepper

Cook spinach according to package directions. Drain. Sauté onion in 1 tablespoon butter. Beat eggs slightly and mix with remaining ingredients. Stir in spinach and onion. Bake in greased 2½-quart casserole in 350° oven 40-45 minutes, or until center is set.

RICE-NUT CASSEROLE

1 pound mushrooms, sliced
1 bunch green onions, sliced
2 cloves garlic, minced
1 stick butter
1¼ cups uncooked brown rice
½ teaspoon salt

¼ teaspoon thyme
⅛ teaspoon pepper
1 cup broken pecan pieces
2 cans (10¾ oz.) condensed beef broth
   mixed with ½ can water

Sauté mushrooms, onions, and garlic in butter in Dutch oven. Stir in rice and cook, stirring until rice is hot—approximately 3 minutes. Add thyme, salt, and pepper. Stir in broken pecans. Pour in beef broth. Heat to boiling. Bake in 400° oven, covered, until liquid is absorbed and rice is tender, approximately 1 hour and 20 minutes.

SPECIAL OCCASION POTATOES

4 baking potatoes
4 tablespoons butter
½ teaspoon pepper
1 teaspoon salt

4 tablespoons grated cheddar cheese
2 tablespoons cream
Grated Parmesan
½ cup finely chopped walnuts

Bake potatoes. When done, cut in half and scoop out meat. Blend with butter, seasonings, cheese, and cream. Heap mixture back into potato shells. Dot with butter and sprinkle with parmesan and walnuts. Return to oven and bake at 375° about 15 minutes, or until nicely browned.

SPICY CARROTS

2 pounds carrots
1¼ cups tomato juice
½ cup vinegar
1 cup sugar substitute

1 tablespoon Worcestershire
1 teaspoon prepared mustard
1 chopped onion
1 chopped green pepper

Peel carrots and slice crosswise. Cook until tender. Drain; add other ingredients. Bring to a boil, cool, and store in refrigerator.

BROCCOLI-POTATO CASSEROLE

2 10-oz. packages frozen chopped broccoli
1 10¾ oz. can potato soup, condensed
½ pint sour cream

Parmesan cheese
2-oz. jar chopped pimiento

Prepare broccoli according to package directions. Drain and cool. Mix soup, sour cream, and broccoli together. Add pimiento. Pour into a 1½-quart casserole. Sprinkle with Parmesan cheese. Bake at 300° for 1 hour.

LIMAS AND MUSHROOMS

½ pound fresh mushrooms
2 tablespoons + 1 teaspoon butter
1 tablespoon finely chopped green onions
1 cup half-and-half

1 tablespoon flour
2 cups cooked fresh or frozen lima beans
¼ teaspoon salt
⅛ teaspoon pepper

Clean and slice the mushrooms. Melt butter in a saucepan. Add onions and cook until soft. Add mushrooms and cook until moisture has evaporated. Add cream and cook until liquid is reduced to ½ cup. Cream 1 tablespoon butter with flour and add to the cream mixture, stirring to blend well. Add limas and bring to a boil. Season with salt and pepper.

TOMATO RICE BAKE

2½ cups peeled tomatoes, chopped
1 tablespoon finely chopped green pepper
1 medium-sized onion, chopped fine
4 strips bacon

1 teaspoon paprika
1 clove garlic
⅛ teaspoon pepper
2½ cups cooked rice (not Minute Rice)

Fry bacon until crisp. Remove from pan. Add onion, tomatoes, green pepper, salt, paprika, garlic, and pepper. Cook until vegetables are transparent. Fold in rice and crumbled bacon. Pour in a casserole and bake for 10 minutes at 350°.

CAULIFLOWER-ONION AU GRATIN

1 medium cauliflower	⅛ teaspoon pepper
2 teaspoons salt	1¼ cups milk
1½ cups small onions	⅓ lb. grated cheddar cheese
½ stick margarine	1 teaspoon Worcestershire
¼ cup flour	

Cook onions in boiling water until tender. Break cauliflower into flowerets and soak in cold water for 1 hour. Cover with water and 1 teaspoon salt and boil for about 10 minutes or until slightly tender. Drain. Place a layer of cauliflower in casserole, then a layer of onions. Melt the margarine and add flour, blending well. Add milk, stirring well. Add salt and pepper. Stir in cheese and Worcestershire sauce and pour over layers of onion and cauliflower. Bake for 30 to 40 minutes at 350°.

THREE VEGETABLE PARMESAN

(Use fresh, frozen, or canned vegetables.)

2 cups cooked peas	½ cup chopped green pepper
2 cups cooked green lima beans	½ cup sour cream
2 cups French-style green beans	½ cup mayonnaise
	1 cup grated Parmesan cheese

Drain the peas, beans, and mix. Add remaining ingredients except cheese and mix well. Pour into a casserole and sprinkle with Parmesan. Bake at 350° for 45 minutes. 8 servings.

PEANUTTY POTATOES

Whip crunchy peanut butter into hot mashed potatoes just before serving.

CHANTILLY POTATOES

6 large potatoes	Freshly ground pepper
¼ cup milk	Salt to taste
½ cup whipping cream	4 tablespoons grated Parmesan cheese
2 tablespoons margarine	Paprika

Peel and wash potatoes and cook in boiling salted water until done. Drain and mash with butter and milk, beating until light and fluffy. (Instant potatoes can be used.) Season with salt and pepper. Pour into a buttered casserole; cover with the cream, which has been whipped until stiff. Sprinkle with cheese and paprika. Bake at 350° until brown on top. Serves 8-10.

FRIED BANANAS

2 firm bananas	¼ cup bread crumbs
1 egg	Dash nutmeg
¼ cup vegetable oil	

Peel and slice bananas into one-inch pieces. Sprinkle with nutmeg. Put egg in small bowl and beat well. Heat oil in skillet over high heat. Dip banana pieces in egg and then roll in bread crumbs. Drop into hot oil and fry until golden brown. Serve hot. Serves 4.

JALAPENO LIMAS

2½ cups cooked lima beans
2 tablespoons butter
¼ cup minced onion

1 cup Jalapeno cheese, grated
Salt and pepper to taste

Melt butter and sauté onion. Stir cheese into onion mixture, over low heat, until melted. Add beans and salt and pepper. Place in a casserole and bake for about ½ hour at 350°. 4 servings.

CASSEROLE BEETS

12 medium-sized fresh beets, peeled and sliced
¼ cup honey
¾ teaspoon salt
¼ teaspoon paprika

3 tablespoons butter
1 tablespoon lemon juice
½ cup water
1 medium-sized onion, grated

Layer slices of beets and onion in casserole dish. Pour honey and salt over them, and sprinkle with paprika. Dot with butter. Add lemon juice, mixed with water and bake, covered, for 30 minutes. 6 servings.

TURNIPS

Peel and slice 7 medium-sized turnips. Cover with cold water. Add a beef bouillon cube, a dash of red pepper flakes, and 1 tablespoon sugar. Cover with water and cook over medium heat until tender. 6 servings.

ORANGE SWEET POTATOES

6 baked sweet potatoes
¼ cup butter
1 cup orange juice
1 tablespoon corn starch

½ cup sugar
¼ teaspoon salt
¾ cup brown sugar

Blend cornstarch, sugar, salt, and brown sugar thoroughly. Combine butter and orange juice and heat. Stir starch mixture into hot juice. Cook and stir about 5 minutes, or until mixture thickens. Peel and slice baked potatoes in ¾-inch slices. Pour syrup over potatoes. Bake 40 minutes in 350° oven. Garnish with orange slices if desired.

CARROT-LIMA-SQUASH MEDLEY

1 cup sugar
2 tablespoons + 2 teaspoons cornstarch
4 teaspoons salt
½ teaspoon dillweed
2⅔ cups orange juice

2 pounds carrots, peeled and diagonally
   sliced (about 6 cups)
4 cups fresh lima beans
2 medium zucchini, sliced
2 medium yellow squash, sliced

Combine sugar, cornstarch, salt, and dillweed in a small saucepan; mix well. Stir in orange juice. Cook over medium heat, stirring constantly, until thickened and bubbly. Reduce heat to low to keep sauce warm.

Steam carrots 10 minutes; add limas and squash. Steam 10 to 15 minutes or until tender. Serve sauce over vegetables. Makes 20-24 servings.

FRIED SWEET POTATOES

Boil sweet potatoes until done. Peel and mash. Season to taste with sugar and salt. Add a little flour to hold together for molding. Dip hands in cold water. Put a miniature marshmallow in the center of each ball—about the size of a golf ball. Roll in corn flakes and fry in deep fat.

ONIONS PARMESAN

2 pounds medium onions	⅛ teaspoon pepper
Butter or margarine	½ teaspoon seasoned salt
½ cup shredded Parmesan cheese	¼ teaspoon Worcestershire
2 tablespoons flour	1 cup half-and-half
2 teaspoons salt	Paprika

Cut peeled, washed onions into rings, ¼-inch thick. In lightly buttered skillet, place half of onions in 3 rows. Top with half of cheese; then rest of onions, then cheese.

Mix flour, salt, pepper, seasoned salt, Worcestershire, and half-and-half until smooth. Pour over onions. Cook, covered, over low heat for 40-50 minutes, or until tender-crisp. Dust with paprika. Serves 6.

TEXAS POTATOES

2-pound bag frozen hash brown potatoes	½ lb. grated cheddar cheese
1 large onion, chopped	1 package herb stuffing mix
2 cans cream of chicken soup (condensed)	8 oz. cream cheese
1 pint sour cream	

Mix potatoes and onions. Place in large baking dish (greased) at least 13 × 19 inches or larger. Mix soup, cream cheese, and sour cream; pour over potatoes. Sprinkle with cheese. Top with stuffing mix, tossed with melted margarine. Bake at 350° for 1½ hours. (Can be less baking time if potatoes are thawed.)

APPLE YAMS

8-10 large, firm green apples	1 20-oz. can sweet potatoes
¼ cup butter	1 teaspoon salt
16 miniature marshmallows	1 tablespoon lemon juice
½ cup dark corn syrup	¼ teaspoon cinnamon
¼ cup melted butter	

Prepare apple shells by scooping out the fruit till wall of apple is ½ inch thick. Mix other ingredients and stuff apples generously. Place stuffed apples in 350 degree oven. Bake ½ hour, till soft but not mushy. 8-10 servings.

OLIVE'S CARROT AND CHEESE RING

3 eggs	2½ cups grated Velveeta cheese
3 cups grated carrots	¼ cup milk

Mix and pour into ring. Place ring in pan of water and bake at 350 degrees for 45 minutes, or until firm.

Serve hot with ring filled with French green beans or peas.

GREEN BEANS AU GRATIN

4 pounds fresh green beans	6 cups milk
1 cup butter or margarine	2 cups shredded Swiss cheese
1 cup all-purpose flour	6 tablespoons grated Parmesan cheese
1 tablespoon + 1 teaspoon salt	Paprika
1 teaspoon dry mustard	2 cups slivered almonds

Remove strings from green beans; cut beans into 1½-inch pieces, and wash thoroughly. Cook beans, covered, in lightly salted water until tender (about 20 to 25 minutes); drain and set aside.

Melt butter in a heavy saucepan over low heat. Blend in flour, salt, and mustard; cook 1 minute, stirring constantly. Gradually add milk; cook over medium heat, stirring, until thickened and bubbly. Stir in Swiss cheese; cook over low heat until cheese is melted.

Combine cheese sauce and beans; spoon into a lightly greased steam table pan. Sprinkle with Parmesan cheese and paprika.

Bake at 350° for 20 minutes. Top with almonds, and bake 5 to 10 minutes or until bubbly. Makes 24 servings.

DILLY GREEN BEANS

8 hard-cooked eggs	2 tablespoons salt
6 pounds fresh green beans	2 tablespoons dillseeds
4 cups chopped onion	Dash of pepper
1 cup butter or margarine, melted	

Cut hard-cooked eggs in half and remove yolk. Chop egg whites and sieve egg yolks; set aside.

Remove strings from beans; cut beans into 2-inch pieces, and wash thoroughly. Cook beans, covered, in lightly salted water until tender (about 20 to 25 minutes); drain well and set aside.

Sauté onion in butter until tender. Add green beans and seasonings, tossing lightly. Cook over medium heat until heated thoroughly. Remove from heat; garnish with chopped egg whites and sieved egg yolks. Makes 16-24 servings.

POTATOES GOURMET

18 medium potatoes	9 green onions, chopped
⅓ cup melted butter or margarine	1 tablespoon salt
6 cups (8 ounces) shredded cheddar cheese	¾ teaspoon pepper
3 8-oz. cartons commercial sour cream	6 tablespoons butter or margarine

Cover potatoes with salted water, and bring to a boil; reduce heat, and cook about 30 minutes or until tender. Cool slightly. Peel and coarsely shred potatoes; set aside.

Combine ¼ cup melted butter and cheese in a heavy saucepan; cook over low heat, stirring constantly, until cheese is partially melted.

Combine potatoes, cheese mixture, sour cream, onion, salt, and pepper; stir well. Spoon potato mixture into a greased steam table pan; dot with 2 tablespoons butter. Cover and bake at 300° for 25 minutes. Makes 18-24 servings.

JALAPENO HOT RICE

6 medium onions, chopped (about 3 cups)
6 medium green peppers, chopped
12 Jalapeno peppers, seeded and finely chopped
1½ cups butter or margarine, melted

6 4-oz. cans mushroom stems and pieces, undrained
6 10¾-oz. cans chicken broth, undiluted
6 cups uncooked rice

Sauté onion, green pepper, and Jalapeno pepper in butter in a medium saucepan until tender. Add mushrooms, chicken broth, and rice; cover and simmer 15 to 20 minutes or until rice is tender. Makes 24 servings.

BAKED CHEESE GRITS

18 cups water
3 tablespoons salt
4½ cups uncooked regular grits
1½ cups butter or margarine

12 cups shredded medium-sharp cheddar cheese, divided
18 eggs, beaten

Combine water and salt; bring to a boil. Stir in grits; cook until done, following package directions. Remove from heat. Add butter and 11¼ cups cheese; stir until completely melted. Add a small amount of hot grits to eggs, stirring well; stir egg mixture into remaining grits. Pour grits into a lightly greased steam table pan; sprinkle with remaining ¾ cup cheese. Bake at 350° for 1 hour and 15 minutes. Makes 18-24 servings.

CHILLED BEETS AND CAULIFLOWER

6 medium heads cauliflower
3 pounds fresh beets

Russian mayonnaise
Minced parsley

Wash cauliflower and break into flowerets. Cook, covered, in a small amount of boiling salted water, about 10 minutes or until done; drain and cool.

Leave root and 1 inch of stem on beets; scrub with a brush. Place beets in a saucepan; add water to cover. Bring to a boil; cover and cook 35 to 40 minutes or until tender. Drain; pour cold water over beets, and drain. Cool. Trim off beet roots and stems, and rub off skins. Dice and add Russian mayonnaise. Mix well, and set aside.

Place cauliflower in a serving bowl; spoon beet mixture over top. Sprinkle with parsley, and chill at least 30 minutes before serving. Makes 24 servings.

SWEET POTATOES WITH COCONUT

16 pounds sweet potatoes
½ pound butter or margarine
1¼ cups sugar

1¼ teaspoons salt
2 tablespoons cinnamon
2 pounds grated coconut

Clean potatoes thoroughly. Place on sheet pans and bake approximately 45 minutes, or until tender. Cut potatoes and scoop out pulp, discarding skin. Put through food mill and thoroughly blend in all remaining ingredients, except coconut. Place in clean pans and refrigerate until firm. With No. 8 ice cream scoop, and portion scale, weigh out 50 4-oz. portions. Form into round, flat patties. Roll in coconut. Place on brown paper on sheet pan and refrigerate until ready to cook. Sauté lightly in butter, or margarine, turning when brown. Remove to sheet pans and finish heating in 350° oven for 10 to 20 minutes. Makes 50 servings of 4 ounces each.

BEETS AND APPLES

3 pounds fresh beets
6 medium apples, peeled, cored, and cut into
    rings
1½ cups firmly packed light brown sugar

3 tablespoons all-purpose flour
3 teaspoons salt
3 tablespoons vinegar
¼ cup butter or margarine

Leave root and 1 inch of stem on beets; scrub with a brush. Place beets in a saucepan; add water to cover. Bring to a boil; cover and cook 35 to 40 minutes or until tender. Drain, reserving 1½ cups juice; pour cold water over beets, and drain.

Trim off beet stems and roots, and rub off skins; cut beets into ¼-inch slices. Place half the beets in a steam table pan; spread half the apples on top. Repeat layers, and set aside.

Combine sugar, flour, salt, vinegar, butter, and reserved beet juice in a small saucepan; cook over medium heat until sugar is melted. Pour over apples and beets; bake at 350° for 20 minutes. Makes 24 servings.

HOLIDAY POTATOES AND PEAS

½ cup butter or margarine
½ cup all-purpose flour
2 teaspoons salt
¼ teaspoon pepper
4½ cups milk

2 cups shredded sharp cheddar cheese
2 10-oz. packages frozen green peas
6 cups sliced cooked potatoes
1 4-oz. jar chopped pimiento
Buttered bread crumbs

Melt butter in a saucepan over low heat; blend in flour, salt, and pepper. Gradually stir in milk, and cook until smooth and thickened, about 5 minutes. Remove from heat; add cheese, stirring until smooth.

Cook peas in lightly salted boiling water until tender but still crisp; drain and combine with potatoes and pimiento in a lightly greased 3-quart casserole. Pour cheese sauce over top and sprinkle with bread crumbs. Bake at 325° for 50 to 60 minutes. Makes 12 servings.

BETTY'S RAINBOW RICE

¼ stick margarine (melted)
2¼ cups converted rice
¼ package home-size onion soup mix
½ cup dehydrated green bell peppers

¼ cup dehydrated red bell peppers
½ large onion, cut into rings
Salt and pepper to taste
¼ 4-oz. jar pimientos, cut into strips

Melt butter in pan. Pour rice in and brown slightly. Add soup mix and peppers, onions, salt, and pepper to taste. Fill pan to about ⅔ full with water. Cover and bake at 350° for 40 minutes or until water is evaporated. About 5 minutes before removal from oven add pimiento strips.

MRS. HOUGH'S SNAP BEANS

¾ cup margarine
3 cups brown sugar

3 small cans frozen limeade
1 #10 can Blue Lake cut green beans,
    drained

Melt margarine and mix well with brown sugar. Add melted limeade. Pour over the *drained beans* and let marinate overnight or longer. Be sure all beans are covered with the liquid. Stir once or twice. Just before serving heat to boiling point. Do not cook. Makes 20 servings.

MARY LOU'S SQUASH

7 cups fresh summer squash, sliced ¼" thick (or
equivalent of frozen)
1 cup chopped onion
⅓ cup diced bell pepper
1 bag herb-seasoned stuffing mix
3 eggs, slightly beaten
2 cans cream of celery soup
2 teaspoons Worcestershire sauce
1 teaspoon salad mustard
1½ teaspoons seasoned salt

¼ teaspoon nutmeg
¼ teaspoon white pepper
½ pound medium cheddar cheese
(grated); reserve ½ cup for topping
3-4 oz. can pimiento, chopped
4 tablespoons crumbled crisp bacon
(optional)
Mushrooms (diced), if desired
Paprika

Cook squash, onion, and bell pepper in unsalted water or chicken broth. When barely tender, mash slightly. Add cheese and all but ¾ cup of the stuffing mix; add pimiento, bacon, and mushrooms.

Mix soup with eggs, mustard, Worcestershire sauce, and seasonings. Pour over squash and mix well. Pour into well-greased baking dish (this fills a large one) and bake for 1 hour at 325°. The reserved cheese and herb stuffing mix should be mixed together and sprinkled over the top and then the paprika should be liberally applied.

SARA ANN'S POTATOES

3 cups thinly sliced potatoes
1 cup thinly sliced onions
2 teaspoons salt
¼ teaspoon pepper

2 tablespoons all-purpose flour
¼ cup margarine
1 cup scalded milk

Grease 1½ quart pyrex pan. Alternate layers of potatoes and onions. Sprinkle each layer with salt, pepper, and flour. Dot with margarine. Pour milk over all. Bake covered at 325 degrees for 1½ hours. Uncover and bake an additional 30 minutes.

BROCCOLI-CHEESE DELIGHT

2 tablespoons butter or margarine
2 tablespoons all-purpose flour
2 cups milk
1 3-oz. package cream cheese, cubed
½ cup shredded Swiss cheese
1 teaspoon salt
⅛ teaspoon ground nutmeg

⅛ teaspoon pepper
1 16-oz. package frozen shredded hash
brown potatoes, thawed
1 10-oz. package frozen chopped
broccoli, cooked and drained
¼ cup dry bread crumbs
1 tablespoon melted butter or margarine

Melt 2 tablespoons butter in a heavy Dutch oven over low heat; add flour and cook 1 minute, stirring constantly. Gradually add milk; cook over medium heat, stirring constantly, until thickened and bubbly. Add cream cheese, Swiss cheese, salt, nutmeg, and pepper; cook over low heat, stirring constantly, until cheese melts. Add potatoes, and stir well.

Spoon one-half of potato mixture into a lightly greased 9-inch square baking dish; spread broccoli evenly over potatoes. Spoon remaining potatoes over broccoli layer. Cover and bake at 350° for 35 minutes.

Combine bread crumbs and 1 tablespoon melted butter, stirring to coat bread crumbs; sprinkle over casserole. Bake, uncovered, an additional 10 to 15 minutes. Makes 8 servings.

EASY POTATO CASSEROLE

3 32-oz. packages, frozen shredded hash brown
   potatoes, thawed
3 medium onions, chopped
1½ cups chopped green pepper
3 10¾-oz. cans cream of potato soup, undiluted

3 10¾-oz. cans cream of celery soup,
   undiluted
3 8-oz. cartons commercial sour cream
1½ teaspoons salt
⅜ teaspoon pepper
3 cups 4-oz. shredded Monterey Jack
   cheese

Combine all ingredients except cheese; stir well. Spoon potato mixture into 3 greased shallow 2-quart casseroles. Bake at 325° for 1 hour and 15 minutes. Sprinkle with cheese and bake an addtional 15 minutes. Makes 24 servings.

OLIVE POTATOES

2¼ cups evaporated milk
2¼ cups water
9 tablespoons butter or margarine
9 tablespoons all purpose flour
12 oz. sharp cheddar cheese, diced
1½ teaspoons salt

Dash of pepper
12 cups diced cooked potatoes
1½ cups sliced ripe olives
1½ cups soft bread crumbs
6 tablespoons melted butter or
   margarine

Combine milk and water; stir well, and set aside.

Melt 9 tablespoons butter in a heavy saucepan over low heat; add flour and cook 1 minute, stirring constantly. Gradually add milk mixture. Add cheese and cook over medium heat, stirring constantly, until thickened and bubbly. Stir in salt and pepper.

Combine potatoes and olives; spoon into 3 lightly greased deep 1½ quart casseroles. Pour cheese sauce over potatoes.

Combine bread crumbs and 6 tablespoons melted butter, stirring to coat bread crumbs; sprinkle evenly over casserole. Bake at 350° for 35 minutes or until bread crumbs are golden. Makes 24 servings.

GREEN BEANS IN SOUR CREAM

6 pounds fresh green beans
3 medium onions, thinly sliced
6 tablespoons finely chopped parsley
6 tablespoons butter or margarine, melted
6 tablespoons all-purpose flour

2 tablespoons grated lemon rind
1 tablespoon salt
¾ teaspoon pepper
3 cups commercial sour cream
3 cups buttered bread crumbs

Remove strings from green beans; cut beans into 1½-inch pieces, and wash thoroughly. Cook beans, covered, in lightly salted water until tender (about 20 to 25 minutes); drain and set aside.

Sauté onion and parsley in butter; reduce heat and add flour, lemon rind, salt, and pepper. Cook, stirring, until bubbly. Add sour cream, and cook just until heated thoroughly.

Combine sour cream mixture and beans; stir well. Spoon beans into a greased steam table pan. Sprinkle bread crumbs over beans. Bake at 350° for 20 minutes. Makes 18-24 servings.

HAWAIIAN BAKED BEANS AND FRANKS

1 #10 can baked beans
3 pounds frankfurters, cut into 1-inch pieces
4½ cups drained crushed pineapple
6 tablespoons finely chopped onion

6 tablespoons brown sugar
3 tablespoons catsup
1 tablespoon prepared mustard

Combine all ingredients; stir well. Spoon mixture into three 2-quart casseroles. Bake, uncovered, at 350° for 50 to 60 minutes. Makes 18-24 servings.

BEEFY BAKED BEANS

5 pounds ground beef
2½ cups chopped onion
1 #10 can pork and beans
2½ cups catsup
5-10 tablespoons vinegar

5 tablespoons Worcestershire sauce
2½ teaspoons salt
1¼ teaspoons pepper
1¼ teaspoons hot sauce

Cook ground beef and onion until meat is browned, stirring to crumble meat. Drain well.

Combine beef mixture and remaining ingredients; stir well. Spoon bean mixture into five 1½ quart casseroles. Bake, uncovered, at 350° for 30 minutes. Makes 20-30 servings.

NEW POTATOES WITH LEMON-CHIVES

12-15 pounds cooked and peeled new potatoes
1½ pounds margarine
1 cup minced chives
½ cup lemon juice

2 cups sour cream
2 tablespoons sugar
2 to 3 tablespoons salt
3 teaspoons black pepper

Place potatoes over medium heat and allow them to heat thoroughly. Melt the margarine in a large saucepan; stir in seasoning, lemon juice, and chives. Keep the mixture warm. Drain the potatoes. Add the sour cream to the butter mixture and pour over the potatoes. Shake the kettle to distribute the sauce and to coat each potato. Lift them out of the sauce and serve hot. Makes 50 servings.

SQUASH CASSEROLE

30 large yellow squash
12 tablespoons butter or margarine, softened
6 cups shredded cheddar cheese
6 medium onions, chopped
3 cups chopped celery
18 slices bacon, cooked, drained, and crumbled
6 2-oz. jars diced pimiento

6 tablespoons chopped green chilies
3 teaspoons salt
1½ teaspoons garlic salt
¾ teaspoon pepper
3 cups soft bread crumbs
6 tablespoons butter or margarine, melted

Wash squash thoroughly; trim off ends. Place in boiling salted water to cover. Cook 15 to 20 minutes or until tender; drain and mash.

Combine next 10 ingredients; add squash, stirring well. Spoon squash mixture into a buttered steam table pan. Combine bread crumbs and 6 tablespoons melted butter; sprinkle over squash mixture. Bake at 350° for 20 minutes. Makes 24-36 servings.

SHIRLEY'S SPINACH

2 pounds frozen spinach, chopped
½ pound margarine

1 pound cream cheese
1 teaspoon lemon juice

Cook spinach and drain well. Melt margarine. Beat cream cheese until smooth. Add margarine and lemon juice. Place drained spinach in shallow steam table pans. Pour margarine and cream cheese mixture over spinach and serve.

MARTY'S BROCCOLI AND PEA CASSEROLE

3 pounds broccoli, chopped
¼ #10 can peas, drained
1 cup onion, chopped
¼ tall can cream of mushroom soup

1¼ cups mayonnaise
1¼ cups grated cheddar cheese
Salt and pepper to taste
⅝ cup Ritz cracker crumbs

Cook broccoli in salty water. Drain. Place half of broccoli in buttered steam table pan. Place peas next. Mix onion, soup, mayonnaise, grated cheese, salt, and pepper. Place half of this sauce, then rest of broccoli, then balance of sauce. Sprinkle with cracker crumbs. Bake at 350° until bubbly.

EGGPLANT CASSEROLE

8 to 10 pounds fresh eggplant
Salted water to cover (1 teaspoon salt for each
    quart of water)
1 quart chicken or meat stock
2 cups sour cream

1 quart bread crumbs
1 tablespoon paprika
1 tablespoon black pepper
1 cup margarine, melted

Peel and cut the eggplant crosswise into ¼-inch thick slices. Drop into the boiling water. Cook just until tender, about 10 minutes. Lift out of the water and lay in layers in greased shallow baking pans. Combine the sour cream, chicken stock, melted margarine, and seasonings. Pour over the eggplant and shake the pan to distribute the sauce. Sprinkle with the bread crumbs and bake at 350° for about 40 minutes, or until the mixture is well blended and slightly brown. If mixture becomes too dry, add a little more stock. Grate cheese if desired and sprinkle over the bread crumbs. Return to oven for a few minutes to melt and/or brown. Makes 50 servings.

Variation: For a one-dish meal add 4 pounds of ground, seasoned, and cooked meat to the sauce before pouring over the eggplant.

LIMA BEANS CREOLE

14 cups fresh lima beans
24 slices bacon
1 cup finely chopped onion
8 tablespoons chopped green pepper

4 16-oz. cans whole tomatoes,
    undrained
2 teaspoons salt
½ teaspoon pepper

Cook beans in boiling salted water in a Dutch oven until tender (20 to 30 minutes); drain. Return beans to Dutch oven, and set aside.

Cook bacon until crisp. Remove from skillet, reserving 8 tablespoons drippings; crumble bacon, and set aside. Sauté onion and green pepper in reserved drippings until tender. Stir onion mixture, bacon, and remaining ingredients into beans; cover and simmer 15 minutes. Makes 24 servings.

STUFFED YELLOW SQUASH WITH CHEESE SAUCE

12 large (about 8 pounds) yellow squash
2 pounds ground beef
4 clove garlic, pressed
2 cups uncooked regular rice
4 teaspoons salt

½ teaspoon pepper
4 16-oz. cans stewed tomatoes
2 cups water
Parmesan Cheese Sauce

Wash squash thoroughly; cook in boiling salted water for 8 to 10 minutes or until tender but still firm. Drain and cool slightly. Trim stems. Cut squash in half lengthwise; remove and discard seeds. Set aside.

Cook ground beef and garlic in a large skillet over medium heat until beef is browned, stirring to crumble meat. Add rice, salt, and pepper; cook 2 minutes, stirring constantly. Add tomatoes and water; stir well. Cover; reduce heat to low, and simmer 20 minutes or until rice is done and liquid is absorbed.

Place squash in a steam table pan. Spoon meat mixture into shells; spoon Parmesan Cheese Sauce over meat mixture. Cover tightly with aluminum foil. Bake at 375° for 15 minutes or until squash are heated thoroughly. Makes 24 servings.

PARMESAN CHEESE SAUCE

4 tablespoons butter or margarine
4 tablespoons all-purpose flour
2 cups milk
8 tablespoons grated Parmesan cheese

1 teaspoon dry mustard
½ teaspoon salt
Dash of pepper
Dash of red pepper

Melt butter in a small heavy saucepan over low heat; add flour, stirring until smooth. Cook 1 minute, stirring constantly. Gradually add milk; cook over medium heat, stirring constantly until thickened and bubbly. Stir in cheese, mustard, salt, and pepper; cook, stirring constantly, until cheese is melted. Makes 2 cups.

PARMESAN TOMATOES

8 pounds (about 15 or 16 small) fresh tomatoes,
    peeled and sliced
1 cup melted butter
2 teaspoons dried oregano leaves

1 teaspoon dried basil leaves
2 cups (8 oz.) grated Parmesan cheese
1 teaspoon dried parsley flakes

Arrange tomatoes in a steam table pan. Pour butter over tomatoes; sprinkle with oregano, basil, cheese, and parsley flakes. Bake at 325° for 25 to 30 minutes. Makes 20-24 servings.

APRICOT GLAZED CARROTS

12 cups sliced carrots
9 tablespoons melted butter or margarine
1 cup apricot preserves
¾ teaspoon salt

¾ teaspoon grated orange rind
¾ teaspoon ground nutmeg
6 teaspoons lemon juice

Cook carrots until tender in enough salted water to cover (about 20 minutes); drain. Combine remaining ingredients, stirring until well blended. Spoon over carrots, and toss well. Serve at once. Makes 18-24 servings.

BACON AND EGG STUFFED TOMATOES

30 large tomatoes	30 slices bacon, cooked and crumbled
Salt and pepper	10 tablespoons chopped fresh parsley
30 hard-cooked eggs, chopped	1¼ teaspoons salt
3¾ cups diced celery	1¼ teaspoons pepper
1⅔ cups mayonnaise	Paprika

Wash tomatoes thoroughly. Cut tops from tomatoes; scoop out pulp, leaving shells intact. Chop tomato pulp. Drain tomato shells, and sprinkle cavities with salt and pepper.

Combine tomato pulp, eggs, celery, mayonnaise, bacon, parsley, 1¼ teaspoon salt, and 1¼ teaspoon pepper; stir well. Fill tomato shells with bacon-and-egg mixture. Sprinkle with paprika.

CHEESY SQUASH

21 medium-sized yellow squash	24 slices bacon, cooked, drained, and
1½ teaspoons salt	crumbled
6 eggs, separated	1 cup fine, dry bread crumbs
3 8-oz. cartons commercial sour cream	3 tablespoons butter or margarine,
6 tablespoons all-purpose flour	melted
5¼ tablespoons shredded cheddar cheese	

Wash squash thoroughly; trim off ends. Place in boiling salted water to cover. Cook 15 to 20 minutes or until tender. Drain and cool slightly. Thinly slice squash; sprinkle with salt.

Beat egg yolks until thick and lemon colored; stir in sour cream and flour. Beat egg whites until stiff peaks form; fold into yolk mixture.

Layer half the squash, egg mixture, and cheese in a steam table pan. Sprinkle with all the bacon. Layer remaining squash, egg mixture, and cheese. Combine bread crumbs and butter; sprinkle over top. Bake at 350° for 20 to 25 minutes. Makes 24-30 servings.

HOT FRUIT COMPOTE

1 can applesauce (or more)	2 bananas, sliced
1 can blue plums (remove seeds)	2-3 tablespoons brown sugar
1 can pineapple chunks	⅓ cup chopped pecans

Place one can applesauce in bottom of casserole and up sides of dish. Drain plums and pineaple. Add layer of plums, then pineapple, then bananas. Do not stir. Add more applesauce on top, sprinkle top with brown sugar and nuts.

Bake in moderate oven until hot and bubbly—about 30 minutes. Serve warm with meat course.

Breads

WHOLE WHEAT BANANA MUFFINS

¾ cup whole wheat flour
¾ cup white flour
2 teaspoons baking powder
¾ cup oatmeal
1 egg

¾ cup milk
⅓ cup mashed banana
¼ cup salad oil
¼ cup honey

Combine flours, baking powder, salt, and oatmeal. Stir. Beat egg, stir in milk, banana, salad oil, and honey. Pour into flour mixture and stir until evenly moist. Spoon into greased muffin cups (12) and bake 15 minutes at 400°.

APRICOT COFFEE CAKE

2 cups rice cereal
3 tablespoons sugar
⅛ teaspoon ginger
¼ cup margarine
1½ cups flour
2 teaspoons baking powder

½ teaspoon salt
¼ cup margarine
¾ cup sugar
1 egg
1 17-oz. can apricot halves

Crush rice cereal. Combine with the next three ingredients and mix until crumbly. Stir flour, baking powder, and salt together.

Beat remaining margarine and sugar until well blended. Add egg. Beat well. Stir in ½ cup syrup from apricots. Add flour mixture, mixing well. Spread in greased 8×8×2-inch baking pan. Chop drained apricots and spoon about ¾ cup evenly over batter. Sprinkle with cereal topping and remaining apricots.

Bake at 350° about 45 minutes or until it pulls away from sides of pan. Serve warm if possible.

CRANBERRY BREAD

1 package orange muffin mix
1 egg

1 cup cranberry-orange relish

Combine the muffin mix with egg and relish until just blended, but lumpy. Pour into a greased loaf pan. Bake at 350° for about 45 minutes, or until brown.

FRESH APPLE BREAD

1½ cup diced tart apples	2¼ cups flour, sifted
1 tablespoon cinnamon	1 teaspoon cinnamon
2 tablespoons brown sugar	½ teaspoon salt
3 tablespoons butter	3½ teaspoons baking powder
⅓ cup butter	¼ cup brown sugar
½ cup brown sugar	2 teaspoons cinnamon
1 egg, beaten	½ teaspoon ground cloves
¾ cup evaporated milk	

Peel, core, and dice apples and sprinkle with cinnamon and sugar. Melt 3 tablespoons butter and add apples. Cover and steam 2 or 3 minutes over low heat.

Cream the butter and sugar until smooth; then add the egg and evaporated milk. Sift flour with cinnamon, salt, and baking powder. Combine the two mixtures and blend. Fold in apples. Pour into a greased and floured 8 × 11-inch pan and sprinkle the top with mixed sugar, cinnamon, and clove. Bake 25 or 30 minutes at 350°. Delicious served hot with sweet cream butter.

LEMON TEA BREAD

1 box lemon cake mix	½ cup salad oil
1 3¾-oz. package instant lemon pudding mix	1 cup cold water
4 eggs	1 oz. poppy seed

Mix cake mix, pudding mix, and poppy seed in a mixing bowl. Add eggs, oil, and water, and beat well. Pour into two 9 × 5-inch loaf pans (well greased) and bake at 350° for 45 to 55 minutes.

PEANUT CORNBREAD

1 12-oz. package corn muffin mix	⅔ cup salted peanuts
⅔ cup milk	3 tablespoons grated Parmesan cheese
1 egg	Dash paprika

Combine muffin mix, milk, and slightly beaten egg. Pour into a greased 9 × 14-inch pan. Sprinkle peanuts over top and press into batter. Sprinkle with cheese. Bake at 400° until golden brown; then sprinkle with paprika. Cut into squares.

LEMON COFFEE CAKE

4 cups biscuit mix	1 egg, well beaten
¾ cup dark brown sugar	6 tablespoons melted butter or
¼ teaspoon nutmeg	margarine
1 teaspoon cinnamon	1 teaspoon grated lemon rind
1¼ cup milk	¼ cup chopped walnuts

Combine biscuit mix, ¼ cup brown sugar, and spices. Mix well. Combine milk, egg, and ¼ cup butter; mix and then add to dry ingredients. Beat well. Mix remaining brown sugar, lemon peel, and walnuts. Pour half the batter into a greased 9 × 9-inch baking pan. Pour 1 tablespoon butter over mixture and sprinkle with half walnut mixture. Pour remaining batter over the mixture, and drizzle with remaining butter and walnut mixture. Bake in 350° oven for about 35 minutes or until done. Serve warm.

TEXAS CORNBREAD

1 package cornbread mix
1 9-oz. can cream-style corn
⅓ cup canned green chilies

2 tablespoons bacon drippings
1 cup shredded sharp processed cheese

Remove seeds from chilies, and rinse well with cold water. Cut into strips and dry on paper towel. Prepare the cornbread mix according to package directions and stir in the corn and bacon drippings. Spoon half the batter into a greased 9×9×2-inch pan. Place chilies over batter and sprinkle with half the cheese. Cover with remaining batter; then add remaining cheese. Bake according to package directions.

SOUR CREAM WAFFLES

1 cup sifted flour
1½ teaspoons sugar
1 teaspoon baking powder
¼ teaspoon soda
¼ teaspoon salt

1 egg
1 cup sour cream
¼ cup milk
3 tablespoons melted butter

Sift dry ingredients together. Beat egg yolk, sour cream, milk, and butter and add to dry ingredients. Beat until smooth. Beat egg whites until stiff; then fold into other mixture. Bake in a hot waffle iron.

HONEY WHEAT BISCUITS

1 cup whole wheat flour
1 cup white flour
4 teaspoons baking powder
¼ teaspoon salt

¼ cup shortening
1 tablespoon honey
½ to ⅔ cup water

Mix flours, baking powder, and salt. Cut in shortening until mixture is consistency of cornmeal. Add the honey and enough water to make a soft dough. Mix well. Roll out on floured board to ½-inch thickness. Cut with a biscuit cutter (use a juice glass, floured, if you don't have a biscuit cutter) and place on a cookie sheet. Bake at 400° until brown (about 15 minutes).

QUICK BANANA NUT BREAD

¼ cup shortening
1 cup sugar
2 eggs

1 cup crushed ripe bananas
2 cups biscuit mix
¼ cup chopped walnuts

Cream sugar and shortening. Add other ingredients and beat until well mixed. Pour into a well-greased loaf pan and bake at 350° for 1 hour. Remove from pan and cool on rack before slicing.

SCALDED CORN CAKES

1 pint boiling water
1 level teaspoon salt

1¾ cups plain corn meal

Add salt to boiling water. Gradually mix in meal. Set in refrigerator for 20 minutes. Place 1 inch of oil in skillet and heat to 350°. Drop corn mixture by spoonfuls into hot oil and fry for about 5 minutes or until golden brown. Makes 18 corn cakes.

SWEET CREAM BISCUITS

4 cups sifted flour
1 teaspoon salt
2 tablespoons baking powder

1½ cups heavy cream
4 tablespoons water (if needed)

Sift together flour, salt, and baking powder. Stir in cream with fork until all flour is moistened. Add water if mixture is too dry. Knead about 10 times, roll to ¾-inch thickness, and cut with small cutter. Bake on ungreased baking sheet in 450° oven for about 12 minutes.

CASSEROLE DILL BREAD

1 package active dry yeast
¼ cup lukewarm water
1 cup large curd creamed cottage cheese
2 tablespoons sugar
2 teaspoons instant minced onion
1 tablespoon margarine

2 teaspoons dillseed
1 teaspoon salt
¼ teaspoon soda
1 egg, beaten
2¼ to 2½ cups sifted flour

Dissolve yeast in lukewarm water. Heat cottage cheese in saucepan until lukewarm. Add sugar, onion, butter, dillseeds, salt, soda, egg, and yeast to cottage cheese in casserole. Add flour, a little at a time, to make a stiff batter. Beat well after each addition. Cover and let rise in warm place until doubled in size— about 30-40 minutes.

Bake in casserole for 40-50 minutes at 350°. Cover with foil the last 15 minutes of baking to prevent excessive browning. Turn out on rack to cool. Makes 1 round loaf.

ZUCCHINI NUT BREAD

3 cups sifted flour
2 teaspoons cinnamon
1 teaspoon soda
1 teaspoon salt
¼ teaspoon baking powder
3 eggs, well beaten

2 cups sugar
1 cup cooking oil
1 tablespoon vanilla
2 cups grated zucchini squash
½ cup chopped pecans
1 teaspoon flour

Sift together 3 cups flour, cinnamon, soda, salt, and baking powder. Add sugar and oil to eggs, beating well. Add vanilla and dry ingredients. Stir in zucchini.

Combine nuts with 1 teaspoon flour; stir into batter. Pour into 2 greased 8½ × 4½ × 2½-inch loaf pans. Bake at 350° for 1 hour or until bread tests done. Cool in pan.

MARVELOUS MUFFINS

1 cup whole wheat flour
1 teaspoon soda
1½ cups all-bran cereal
½ cup raisins

1 egg, well beaten
½ cup honey
¾ cup milk
2 tablespoons butter, softened

Mix flour, soda, and bran and moisten with mixture of egg, honey, milk, and butter. Add raisins. Stir only enough to blend. Bake in well-greased muffin pan at 400° for 25 minutes. Makes 12.

PUMPKIN BREAD

Sift together in bowl:
3⅓ cups flour
3 cups sugar
2 teaspoons soda
1½ teaspoons salt
1 teaspoon cinnamon
1 teaspoon nutmeg

Make a well in the mixture and add:
1 cup oil
4 eggs
⅔ cup water
2 cups (#303 can) pumpkin

Beat with mixer until smooth. Portion batter into three loaf pans. Bake at 350° for 1 hour or until done.

BREAKFAST BREAD PUDDING

8 slices whole wheat bread, cubed
3 eggs
3 cups milk
¼ cup sugar

2 teaspoons vanilla
¼ teaspoon nutmeg
⅛ teaspoon cinnamon

Place bread in the bottom of a 10 × 6 × 1¾-inch baking dish. Beat eggs with remaining ingredients and pour over bread. Put dish in a larger pan and fill larger pan with 1 inch of hot water. Put in oven and bake 1 hour at 325°. Place under broiler and brown top (about 2 minutes). Makes 6 servings.

PEANUT BUTTER BREAD

4½ cups flour, sifted
6 teaspoons baking powder
1¼ teaspoons salt
⅔ cup sugar
1 cup peanut butter

2 eggs, well beaten
2 cups milk
1 tablespoon grated orange rind
½ cup chopped, salted peanuts

Sift flour with baking powder, salt, and sugar. Cut in peanut butter with two knives or pastry blender until mixture is like corn meal. Combine eggs, milk, and orange rind and stir with chopped peanuts into flour mixture until blended. Grease bottom and sides of loaf pan 10 × 5 × 4 inches. Pour batter into pan. Bake at 350° for one hour—or until done. Remove from pan and cool. Wrap in foil and store overnight before cutting.

WHOLE WHEAT BREAD

1½ cakes yeast
½ cup lukewarm water
1 cup milk, scalded and then cooled
⅓ cup honey

3⅓ cups stone-ground whole wheat
 flour
2 eggs, beaten slightly
¾ teaspoon salt
¼ cup melted butter

Crumble yeast in lukewarm water. Add honey to milk and stir until honey is dissolved. Add milk and honey to beaten eggs; then stir in the salt and melted butter. Pour over the dissolved yeast (but be sure it isn't too hot). Add 2 cups of flour and beat for about 4 minutes. Add remaining flour and beat until dough is spongy. Cover and let rise for 2 to 2½ hours, or until double in bulk. Place in a greased loaf pan and let rise again for 45 minutes to 1 hour. Bake in a 350° oven for 45-50 minutes, or until browned and firm. Note: Stone-ground whole wheat flour can be found in health food stores.

CRANBERRY LEMON NUT BREAD

¼ cup vegetable shortening
¾ cup sugar
1 egg
1⅓ cups milk
3 cups flour
3½ teaspoons baking powder

1 teaspoon salt
1 cup chopped nuts
1 cup fresh cranberries, rinsed and
    drained
Grated rind of 1 lemon
1 teaspoon ground mace

Cream shortening and sugar. Beat in egg. Stir in milk; then add flour, baking powder, and salt; beat well. Fold in nuts, cranberries, lemon rind, and mace. Pour into a greased $9 \times 5 \times 3$-inch loaf pan. Bake in preheated 350° oven for 60-70 minutes or until top is firm and browned. Cool thoroughly before slicing. (Slices better the second or third day.)

SUGAR TOP DATE MUFFINS

3 cups shortening
3 cups sugar
1½ cups brown sugar
12 eggs
¾ cup milk
2¾ pounds flour
¼ cup baking powder

1 tablespoon salt
1 pint reconstituted lemon juice
4 pounds diced dates
½ cup sugar
½ cup brown sugar
2 tablespoons cinnamon

Beat shortening and sugars together in mixer bowl at medium speed until fluffy and creamy. Add eggs and milk and continue beating for 2 minutes. Sift flour, baking powder, and salt together. Add to sugar-egg mixture; beat. Add lemon juice and beat well for about 2 minutes at low speed. Scrape bottom of bowl and sides and beat again until blended. Fold in diced dates. Scale into well-greased muffin pans about ⅔ full. Combine sugar, brown sugar, and cinnamon. Sprinkle over muffin tops. Bake at 375° for 12 to 15 minutes or until well done. Makes 100 medium muffins.

BANANA MUFFINS

½ cup margarine, softened
1 cup sugar
2 eggs beaten

3 ripe bananas, mashed
1¼ cups all-purpose flour
½ teaspoon soda

Combine margarine and sugar; beat until light and fluffy. Add eggs, and beat well. Stir in bananas. Combine flour and soda; add to creamed mixture, stirring just enough to moisten dry ingredients.

Fill muffin pans two-thirds full. Bake at 350° for 25 minutes or until done. Serve hot. Makes about 1¼ dozen.

HOT CHEESE BISCUITS

2 cups all-purpose flour
2 teaspoons baking powder
½ teaspoon salt
½ to ¾ teaspoon red pepper

¼ cup shortening
1 cup shredded sharp cheddar cheese
1 cup buttermilk

Combine flour, baking powder, salt, and red pepper; cut in shortening and cheese until mixture resembles coarse meal. Add buttermilk, stirring until dry ingredients are moistened.

Drop dough by heaping teaspoonfuls about 2 inches apart on lightly greased baking sheets. Bake at 450° for 10 to 12 minutes. Makes about 3 dozen.

WHOLE WHEAT BANANA BREAD

1 cup whole wheat flour
½ cup all-purpose flour
1 teaspoon soda
¾ teaspoon salt
½ cup butter or margarine, softened

¾ cup sugar
1 egg
1¼ cups mashed bananas or 3 small
    bananas, mashed
¼ cup buttermilk

Combine flour, soda, and salt; stir well, and set aside.

Combine butter and sugar; cream mixture until light and fluffy. Add egg, and mix well.

Combine bananas and buttermilk; add to creamed mixture alternately with dry ingredients, stirring only until combined.

Pour batter into a greased and floured 9 × 5 × 3-inch loaf pan. Bake at 350° for 50 minutes or until bread tests done. Cool 10 minutes in pan; remove to wire rack, and cool completely. Makes 1 loaf.

BANANA-SOUR CREAM COFFEE CAKE

½ cup chopped pecans
¼ cup sugar
½ teaspoon ground cinnamon
½ cup shortening
1 cup sugar
2 eggs
1 cup mashed bananas

1 teaspoon vanilla extract
½ cup commercial sour cream
2 cups all-purpose flour
1 teaspoon baking powder
1 teaspoon soda
¼ teaspoon salt

Combine pecans, ¼ cup sugar, and cinnamon; stir well, and set aside.

Combine shortening and 1 cup sugar; cream until light and fluffy. Beat in eggs, bananas, and vanilla; stir in sour cream.

Combine remaining dry ingredients; add to creamed mixture, and stir just enough to blend.

Sprinkle half of reserved cinnamon mixture into bottom of a well-greased 10-inch Bundt pan; spoon half of batter into pan. Sprinkle remaining cinnamon mixture over batter; spoon remaining batter into pan. Bake at 350° for 40 to 45 minutes or until cake tests done.

Cool cake 5 minutes in pan on a wire rack. Loosen edges of cake, if necessary. Invert cake on serving plate; serve warm or cold. Makes one 10-inch coffee cake.

FIG COFFEE CAKE

1½ cups firmly packed brown sugar
6 tablespoons butter or margarine, softened
1½ teaspoons ground cinnamon
30 fig-filled bar cookies, crumbled
6 eggs
2¼ cups sugar
1 cup melted butter or margarine

4½ cups all-purpose flour
1 tablespoon + 1 teaspoon baking
    powder
1½ teaspoons salt
1½ cups milk
1 tablespoon vanilla extract

Combine brown sugar, 6 tablespoons butter, cinnamon, and crumbled fig cookies; mix well, and set aside.

Beat eggs in a large mixing bowl until frothy; add sugar and melted butter. Beat well. Combine flour, baking powder, and salt; gradually add flour mixture to egg mixture alternately with milk, mixing well. Stir in vanilla.

Pour half of batter into a greased and floured square pan; top with half of fig mixture. Pour remainder of batter over fig layer. Sprinkle remaining fig mixture on top in a lattice fashion. Bake at 350° for 40 to 45 minutes or until cake tests done. Makes 27 servings.

CHERRY BLOSSOM COFFEE CAKE

½ cup milk, scalded
⅓ cup sugar
⅓ cup butter
2 teaspoons salt
1 package dry yeast
¼ cup warm water (105° to 115°)

2 eggs
4 cups all-purpose flour
¼ cup softened butter, divided
1 21-oz. can cherry pie filling, divided
¾ cup sugar

Combine milk, ⅓ cup sugar, ⅓ cup butter, and salt; stir until butter melts. Cool to 105° to 115°.

Combine yeast and water; let stand 5 minutes. Stir in milk mixture, eggs, and flour; beat until mixture is smooth and leaves sides of bowl.

Turn dough out onto a floured surface; knead until dough is smooth and elastic (about 5 minutes).

Place dough in a greased bowl, turning to grease top. Cover and let rise in a warm place (85°), free from drafts, 2 to 2½ hours or until doubled in bulk.

Punch dough down, and divide in half. Roll out half the dough into a 24 × 6-inch rectangle. Spread 2 tablespoons softened butter down the center of dough, leaving a 2½-inch margin on each side. Spoon half of cherry pie filling over butter, leaving a 1-inch margin at both ends; sprinkle ¼ cup sugar over cherries. Fold one long side of dough over filling; fold opposite side of dough to overlap. Seal edges.

Place one end of pastry, seam side down, in the center of a well-greased 9-inch round baking pan. Wrap pastry to form a coil. Flatten dough slightly with your hand.

Starting at the center of coil, make deep slashes 1 inch apart along top of dough. Sprinkle 2 tablespoons sugar over dough. Repeat procedure with remaining half of dough. Cover and let rise in a warm place (85°), free from drafts, 1 hour or until doubled in bulk.

Bake at 350° for 35 to 40 minutes or until golden brown. Let cool 15 to 20 minutes before removing from pan. Yield: two 9-inch coffee cakes.

SOUTHERN CRACKLIN' CORNBREAD

4 cups cornmeal
2 teaspoons soda
1½ teaspoons salt
4 eggs, beaten

4 cups buttermilk
⅓ cup bacon drippings
1 cup cracklings

Combine cornmeal, soda, and salt; stir in eggs and buttermilk. Heat bacon drippings in a 13 × 9 × 2-inch baking pan until very hot; add drippings and cracklings to batter, mixing well.

Pour batter into hot pan; bake at 450° for 25 minutes or until bread is golden. Cut into squares. Makes 15 to 20 servings.

FEATHER BISCUITS

1 package dry yeast
2 tablespoons warm water (105° to 115°)
2 cups buttermilk

5 cups self-rising flour
¼ cup sugar
1 cup shortening

Dissolve yeast in warm water. Stir yeast mixture into buttermilk; mix well, and set aside.

Combine flour and sugar; cut in shortening until mixture resembles coarse meal. Add buttermilk mixture; stir until dry ingredients are moistened. Cover and let rise in a warm place until doubled. Or cover bowl tightly, and store in refrigerator until needed. (Dough may be stored up to 3 days.)

Punch dough down; turn dough out on a lightly floured surface. Knead lightly 3 or 4 times.

Roll dough to ½-inch thickness; cut with a 2-inch biscuit cutter. Place biscuits on lightly greased baking sheets; bake at 450° for 10 to 12 minutes or until lightly browned. Makes about 3 dozen biscuits.

COFFEE RING

1 package dry yeast
¼ cup warm water (105° to 115°)
½ cup milk, scalded
¼ cup shortening
¼ cup sugar
½ teaspoon salt
1 egg, slightly beaten
½ teaspoon vanilla extract
1 teaspoon grated lemon rind

2½ to 3 cups all-purpose flour
2 tablespoons melted butter or
    margarine
½ cup raisins
½ cup toasted slivered almonds
⅓ cup sugar
1½ teaspoons ground cinnamon
Glaze (recipe follows)

Dissolve the yeast in warm water, and set aside. Combine milk, shortening, ¼ cup sugar, and salt; stir well. Cool mixture to 105° to 115°.

Combine milk mixture, egg, vanilla, lemon rind, and 1 cup flour; beat until smooth. Stir in yeast mixture; add remaining flour to make a soft dough.

Turn dough out onto a floured surface; knead 8 to 10 minutes or until dough is smooth and elastic. Place dough in a well-greased bowl, turning once to grease top. Cover; let rise in a warm place (85°), free from drafts, until doubled in bulk (about 1½ hours).

Punch dough down; turn out onto a floured surface. Cover dough, and let rest 10 minutes. Roll out dough into a 21 × 7-inch rectangle.

Brush butter evenly over dough, leaving a 1-inch margin. Combine raisins, almonds, ⅓ cup sugar, and cinnamon; sprinkle mixture evenly over dough, leaving a 1-inch margin.

Roll up dough, jellyroll fashion, beginning at long side; pinch edges to seal. Place roll on large, greased cookie sheet, seam side down; shape into a ring, and pinch ends together to seal.

Using kitchen shears, make cuts in dough every inch around ring, cutting two-thirds of the way through roll at each cut. Gently turn each piece of dough on its side, slightly overlapping slices.

Cover; let rise in a warm place (85°), free from drafts, for 45 to 55 minutes or until doubled in bulk. Bake at 375° for 15 to 20 minutes or until golden brown. Transfer to a wire rack; drizzle with glaze while hot. Makes 16 to 20 servings.

GLAZE

1 cup powdered sugar
1 tablespoon + 1 teaspoon milk

½ teaspoon vanilla extract
Dash of salt

Combine all ingredients; stir until smooth. Makes about ½ cup.

CHEESY SAUSAGE BISCUITS

1 pound mild bulk pork sausage
1 small onion, finely chopped
1 11-oz. can cheddar cheese soup, undiluted

½ cup water
3 cups biscuit mix

Crumble sausage into a large skillet; add onion and cook over medium heat until sausage is browned. Drain well on paper towels.

Combine all ingredients, stirring until dry ingredients are moistened. Drop batter by heaping tablespoonfuls about 2 inches apart on lightly greased baking sheets. Bake at 425° for 15 minutes or until lightly browned. Makes about 4 dozen biscuits.

ORANGE ROLLS

1 package dry yeast
¼ cup warm water (105° to 115°)
1 cup milk, scalded
¼ cup sugar
1 teaspoon salt

¼ cup vegetable oil
1 egg, beaten
About 3½ cups all-purpose flour
Orange Butter (recipe follows)

Dissolve yeast in warm water; set mixture aside.

Combine milk, sugar, and salt; stir well. Cool to 105° to 115°.

Combine yeast mixture, milk mixture, oil, and egg; stir well. Add 1¾ cups flour, and beat well. Stir in remaining flour; beat well. Cover and let rise in a warm place (85°), free from drafts, until doubled in bulk.

Punch dough down, and divide in half. Turn dough out onto a heavily floured surface (dough will be very soft). Knead each dough half lightly 6 to 8 times to form a smooth ball.

Place stockinette cover on rolling pin; flour well. Roll out each dough ball to 14 × 9-inch rectangle. Spread ¾ cup Orange Butter evenly over each rectangle, leaving a 1-inch margin.

Roll up rectangles lengthwise; pinch long edges to seal (do not seal ends). Cut into 1½-inch slices. Place rolls, cut side down, in 2 well-greased 9-inch cakepans, leaving about ½ inch space between rolls. Cover and let rise in a warm place (85°), free from drafts, for 30 minutes or until golden brown. Remove rolls from pan while hot. Makes about 2 dozen.

ORANGE BUTTER

½ cup butter or margarine, softened
1 cup sugar

Grated rind of 2 oranges

Combine all ingedients; beat at medium speed of electric mixer until fluffy. Yield: about 1½ cups.

CINNAMON-NUT BREAD

1 cup commercial sour cream
½ cup sugar
2 packages dry yeast
1 teaspoon salt
3 eggs
½ cup butter or margarine, softened
4½ cups all-purpose flour, divided

1 cup sugar
1 cup chopped walnuts
¾ teaspoon ground cinnamon
½ cup melted butter or margarine
1 cup powdered sugar
2 tablespoons milk

Combine sour cream, ½ cup sugar, yeast, and salt; mix well. Add eggs, ½ cup butter, and 2¼ cups flour; beat until mixture is smooth. Add remaining flour; mix well.

Turn dough out onto a floured surface; knead until dough is smooth and elastic (5 to 8 minutes).

Place dough in a greased bowl, turning to grease top. Cover and let rise in a warm place (85°), free from drafts, 1½ to 2 hours or until doubled in bulk.

Punch dough down; turn dough over and cover. Let rise 45 minutes.

Combine 1 cup sugar, walnuts, and cinnamon; stir well. Punch dough down; shape into 1½-inch balls. Dip each in butter; roll in sugar mixture. Layer dough balls in a well-greased 10-inch tube pan (one piece). Cover and let rise in a warm place (85°), free from drafts, 45 minutes or until doubled in bulk.

Bake at 375° for 40 to 50 minutes. Cool bread 10 minutes in pan; invert onto serving platter.

Combine powdered sugar and milk; drizzle over warm bread. Makes one 10-inch coffee cake.

Desserts

DIETERS' CHOICE

1 cup pineapple chunks (no sugar)
2 bananas
½ lb. seedless grapes

2 oranges, peeled with membrane and
    seeds removed
1 cup lemon-lime soda

Slice bananas and dip into juice of pineapple. Layer pineapple, banana slices, and oranges with grapes (stemmed) in center of bowl. Chill thoroughly. Just before serving, pour chilled carbonated beverage over fruit. Makes 4 servings.

OKLAHOMA TARTS

2 cups sifted flour
¾ cups shortening

1 teaspoon salt
6 tablespoons cold water

Filling:

1 cup raisins
1 cup sugar
1 stick butter or margarine

1 cup chopped peanuts
2 eggs, separated
1 teaspoon vanilla

Sift flour and salt into mixing bowl. Cut in shortening with pastry blender until mixture resembles cornmeal. Sprinkle water evenly over mixture. Stir with fork until dough clings together. Roll out on floured board. Cut into 5-inch circles and fit into 3-inch tart shells. Note: Frozen tart shells may be substituted if desired. For filling, cream sugar and margarine and add two egg yolks, nuts, raisins, and 1 teaspoon vanilla. Beat egg whites until stiff and carefully fold into sugar mixture. Put one tablespoon filling into each tart. Bake for 20 minutes at 375°.

YUM-YUM BARS

½ cup butter
1 cup sugar
1 egg
1 egg yolk
1 teaspoon vanilla
1½ cups cake flour

½ teaspoon salt
1 teaspoon baking powder
1 egg white
1 cup light brown sugar (do not pack)
1 cup pecans

Mix first seven ingredients in order and put in 9 × 13 × 2-inch greased pan. Beat egg whites until very stiff. Fold in the brown sugar and pecans. Spread on batter and bake at 300° for 30-35 minutes. Makes 24 bars.

KIDS' DELIGHT PIE

2 eggs
1 cup sugar
½ cup crunchy peanut butter
1 cup light corn syrup
1 teaspoon vanilla

1 unbaked pastry shell
¼ cup melted butter
¾ cup crushed cornflakes
½ cup crushed peanuts
½ cup brown sugar

Beat eggs well. Mix eggs, corn syrup, sugar, peanut butter, and vanilla, beating well. Pour into pie shell and bake at 350° for 45-60 minutes, or until firm. Ten minutes before pie is done, add a topping of ¼ cup melted butter combined with ¾ cup crushed corn flakes, ½ cup chopped peanuts and ½ cup brown sugar. Spread topping over pie and finish baking.

PRALINE COOKIES

1 frothy beaten egg white
1 cup well-packed brown sugar

1½ cups large pecan pieces
1 teaspoon vanilla

Add sugar, nuts, and vanilla to beaten egg white. Drop by spoonfuls on a greased (foil-covered) cookie sheet. Preheat oven to 400°. Place cookies in oven; cut off heat and bake for 8 minutes. Remove from oven and allow cookies to cool on sheet before serving. Makes 2 to 3 dozen.

STEAMED PUDDING

2½ cups sifted flour
3 teaspoons baking powder
½ teaspoon soda
1 teaspoon cinnamon
½ teaspoon ground nutmeg
½ teaspoon allspice

2 cups chopped dates
¼ cup shortening
1 cup sugar
1 egg
1 10¾-oz. can condensed tomato soup

Sift flour with baking powder, soda, and spices. Dust dates with small amount of flour mixture. Cream shortening and sugar; add egg and mix well. Add dry ingredients alternately with soup; stir well after each addition. Fold in dates. Pour into greased 1½-quart casserole. Cover securely with aluminum foil. Place on trivet in large kettle. Add boiling water to one-half height of mold. Cover; steam 2 hours. Remove mold from water; uncover and loosen edges with knife. Unmold while hot. Serve with Hard Sauce.

HARD SAUCE

⅓ cup soft butter
1 cup sifted confectioner's sugar

½ teaspoon vanilla extract

Soften butter; add sugar, a little at a time; and beat until creamy and smooth. Stir in vanilla extract. Chill until hard.

PEACH MELBA

Use fresh or fresh frozen (unsweetened) peaches. Peel and cut into halves. Place a half of a peach in the bottom of each dessert dish, covered with a helping of vanilla ice cream. Top with raspberry sauce, made by puréeing frozen raspberries in the blender.

93

FRESH PEACHES ELEGANTE

Peel and halve fresh peaches. Chill: place halves in a glass bowl; and, just before serving, pour cold catawba grape juice over peaches. Spoon a peach half and some of the juice into dessert dishes at the table.

FRESH BERRIES AND . . .

Serve any fresh berries in sherbet glasses, topped with vanilla ice cream, lemon sherbet, or Hard Sauce (see p. 93).

ROSY CHIFFON CAKE

2¼ cups cake flour
1½ cups sugar
3 teaspoon baking powder
1 teaspoon soda
1½ teaspoons allspice
1 teaspoon ground cinnamon
½ teaspoon ground cloves

1 can (10¾ oz.) condensed tomato soup
½ cup salad oil
5 egg yolks
¼ cup water
1 cup egg whites (7 or 8 eggs)
½ teaspoon cream of tartar

Measure flour, sugar, baking powder, soda, and spices into mixing bowl. Make a well in the mixture. Add soup, oil, egg yolks, and water; beat until smooth. Beat egg whites and cream of tartar together in large mixing bowl until they form *very stiff* peaks. Pour egg yolk mixture gradually over whites, gently folding with rubber spatula until completely blended. Pour into ungreased 10-inch tube pan. Bake at 325° for 65-70 minutes or until top springs back when lightly touched. Remove from oven and let cool for at least one hour. Loosen cake around edge and tube of pan with spatula if needed, and remove from pan. Glaze if desired.

Glaze:

3 tablespoons milk
2 tablespoons butter or margarine
2 cups sifted confectioner's sugar

2 teaspoons grated lemon rind
2 teaspoons lemon juice

Heat milk with butter. Stir into sugar, beating until smooth. Blend in lemon rind and juice.

MARGIE'S RASPBERRY DELIGHT

1 10-oz. package frozen raspberries, thawed
1 cup sugar

2 egg whites
1 12-oz. carton frozen topping

Beat raspberries, sugar, and egg whites for fifteen minutes at top mixer speed. Then blend in whipped topping. Pour over crumbs and freeze.

Crumb Crust:

1 cup flour
½ cup margarine, melted

½ cup chopped nuts
¼ cup brown sugar

Mix and bake in a 9 × 13 pan for 15 minutes at 375°.

When the crumbs have cooled, loosen them and crumble coarsely. Makes 12 servings.

PEACH DELIGHT

Make crumb crust as for Raspberry Delight.

3 eggs	**¼ teaspoon Cream of Tartar**
1 cup sugar	**¼ cup sugar**
3 fresh peaches	**1 12-oz. carton frozen topping**
1 tablespoon lemon juice	

Beat 2 egg yolks and 1 whole egg. Stir in 1 cup sugar, 2 crushed peaches, lemon juice. Stir over low heat until thick. Cool. Beat 2 egg whites until foamy. Add cream of tartar and continue beating. Beat in ¼ cup sugar, a tablespoon at a time, until stiff peaks form. Beat whipped topping (thawed) into egg whites, and fold into cooled egg mixture, along with one sliced peach. Pour over crumb mixture and freeze. Makes 12 servings.

LIME SOUFFLÉ

2 envelopes unflavored gelatin	**2 teaspoons grated lime peel**
½ cup cold water	**8 egg whites**
8 egg yolks	**1 cup granulated sugar**
1 cup lime juice	**2 cups whipping cream, whipped**
1 cup granulated sugar	

Sprinkle gelatin over cold water to soften. In top of a double boiler, combine egg yolks, lime juice, and 1 cup sugar. Cook over boiling water, stirring constantly until mixture coats back of spoon. Stir in dissolved gelatin and lime peel. Turn into 3-quart bowl; refrigerate until slightly thickened; stir occasionally.

Beat egg whites until they hold their shape; gradually beat in 1 cup sugar; continue to beat until mixture holds peaks.

On top of lime mixture, pile stiffly beaten egg whites and whipped cream; gently fold mixture together. Pour into a 6-cup soufflé dish; refrigerate 3 hours or until firm. Makes 12 servings.

CARROT PECAN CAKE

Chop fine in blender and set aside:
    1 cup pecans

Place in blender container:

1¼ cups salad oil	**2 teaspoons cinnamon**
4 eggs	**1 teaspoon salt**
2 cups sugar	

Blend 5 seconds, then add gradually:
    3 cups sliced raw carrots

Blend just until grated.

In large mixing bowl, sift together:

2 cups plain flour	**2 teaspoons baking powder**
1 teaspoon soda	

Pour the contents of the blender over the dry ingredients. Mix well with an electric mixer. Stir in the finely chopped pecans. Pour into greased tube pan. Bake at 325° for about 1 hour and 10 minutes.

CARROT PECAN CAKE ICING

4 tablespoons butter, room temperature
1 8-oz. package cream cheese, room
    temperature
2 cups confectioner's sugar

1 teaspoon vanilla
½ cup coconut, grated
½ cup pecans, chopped

Blend butter and cream cheese. Slowly blend in confectioner's sugar, vanilla, and coconut. Add pecans last, mixing well. Frost the cake.

BAKED ALASKA

As a foundation, bake your favorite one-layer cake. Top with vanilla ice cream, frozen hard. Top with meringue, being careful to cover all of ice cream, and slide under a very hot broiler to brown.

Meringue:

3 egg whites at room temperature
6 tablespoons sugar

½ teaspoon vanilla

Beat egg whites until dry and stiff. Add sugar gradually, 1 tablespoon at a time, beating well after each addition. Continue beating until stiff peaks form when egg beater is lifted. Add vanilla.

MARGARET'S CHINESE CHEWS

¾ cup flour
1 cup sugar
1 cup chopped dates
½ cup coconut

1 cup chopped pecans
1 stick butter, melted
2 eggs, well beaten

Sift together flour and sugar. Add dates, nuts, and coconut. Add eggs. Pour over melted butter and mix well. Bake in a well-buttered 7 × 10 pan for about 30 minutes (until brown) at 350°.

Let cool slightly and then take a teaspoonful at a time and roll into balls. Roll in powdered sugar.

PINEAPPLE ICEBOX DESSERT

Mix together in saucepan 1 small can crushed pineapple, 1 stick butter, 1 cup sugar, 1 tablespoon cream, and one egg, beaten. Bring to a boil and boil slowly for 5 minutes, stirring constantly. Pour over ¾-inch layer of vanilla wafer crumbs in the bottom of each dessert dish. Sprinkle crumbs on top. Refrigerate for 6 hours. Top with whipped cream if desired. Six servings.

GREEN GRAPES IN SOUR CREAM

3 pounds seedless green grapes
1 pint of sour cream

1 cup brown sugar

Wash and stem grapes; drain thoroughly. Pour sour cream over grapes and sprinkle with brown sugar. Mix well and let stand overnight in refrigerator.

ORANGE CANDY COOKIES

1½ cups brown sugar
2 eggs
1 teaspoon soda
½ teaspoon salt
½ cup flaked coconut
½ cup chopped nuts

½ cup rolled oats
½ cup shortening
2 cups sifted flour
½ teaspoon baking powder
1 pound orange slice candy, diced and
    mixed with ½ cup flour

Cream sugar and shortening until light and fluffy. Beat in eggs. Sift flour, soda, baking powder, and salt and blend into creamed mixture. Fold in candy, coconut, nuts, and rolled oats, mixing well. Roll into balls, about 1-inch in diameter. Place on greased baking sheet and press down with the tines of a fork. Bake at 325 for about 12 minutes or until lightly browned.

CHOCOLATE PIE SUPREME

1 stick butter
¾ cup sugar
1½ squares melted unsweetened chocolate
2 eggs

1 teaspoon vanilla
Whipped topping
8-inch pie shell, baked

Combine butter and sugar thoroughly with electric mixer. Add melted chocolate and 1 egg and beat five minutes; add second egg and beat another five minutes; then add vanilla. Pour into baked pie shell and refrigerate several hours. Spread with whipped cream just before serving. Note: Be sure to beat the full five minutes each time.

WHITE FRUITCAKE

1 cup chopped dates, mixed with 1 cup flour
3 cups pecan pieces

¼ pound candied pineapple
½ pound candied cherries

Mix together:
2 cups sugar
½ pound melted butter
1 cup buttermilk, with 1 teaspoon soda added

2 cups flour
1 teaspoon vanilla

Add fruit mix. Beat 5 egg whites. Fold in cake mixture last. Bake at 275° for 1¼ to 1½ hours in greased stem pan.

CHOCOLATE CAKE

2 cups flour
½ cup buttermilk
2 cups sugar
½ teaspoon salt
2 sticks margarine

1 cup water
3 tablespoons cocoa
2 eggs, well beaten
1 teaspoon soda
1 teaspoon cinnamon

Sift flour, measure, and resift with sugar and salt. In a saucepan, put margarine, water, and cocoa. Bring to a boil and pour over flour and sugar mixture. In another bowl, put eggs, soda, buttermilk, cinnamon, and vanilla. Add to above mixture and mix well. Bake in a greased floured pan, about 15½ × 10½. Bake for 20 minutes at 350°. Frost with Fudge Frosting (page 99).

LUCI MAE'S STUFFED PEACHES

18 canned peach halves
9 coconut macaroons or vanilla wafers, crushed
2 tablespoons sugar

¼ cup butter
1 egg yolk
½ teaspoon almond flavoring

Soften butter, crumble cookies, and mix together with egg yolk and sugar. Put a smooth mound over each peach half. Place in buttered pan and bake at 350° for 30 minutes. Serve with baked chicken, turkey, roast pork, or ham. Makes 18 servings.

POT DE CRÈME

1 4-oz. package chocolate pudding mix (not instant)
⅓ cup sugar
1 tablespoon instant coffee powder
1½ cups milk

2 egg yolks, slightly beaten
⅛ teaspoon peppermint extract
½ cup heavy cream

Combine pudding mix, sugar, instant coffee, and milk in saucepan. Cook and stir over medium heat until mixture begins to thicken. Pour a little of the hot mixture into egg yolks and stir quickly to blend. Add to mixture in saucepan and continue cooking until mixture comes to a full boil. Stir in peppermint extract. Cover with wax paper and chill thoroughly. Then whip cream and fold into chilled pudding. Spoon into demitasse cups or sherbet glasses. Chill until set, about two hours. Garnish with whipped cream and shaved chocolate. Makes 8-10 servings—more if served in demitasse cups.

BETTY JO'S CHOCOLATE ANGEL DESSERT

1 12-oz. package semi-sweet chocolate chips
2½ tablespoons water
4 egg yolks
4 egg whites
2 tablespoons confectioner's sugar

½ pint whipping cream, whipped (or
    whipped topping)
1 cup chopped nuts
1 bakery angel food cake

Melt chips in water. Add egg yolks, beating well. Cool while you beat separately egg whites until stiff; add 2 tablespoons confectioner's sugar. Combine the two mixtures; then add whipped cream and nuts. Tear the angel food cake into small pieces and place in a 9 × 13-inch pan. Pour chocolate mixture over the cake. Chill overnight. Cut in squares to serve. Additional whipped topping and a cherry may be used to garnish.

FAVORITE BROWNIES

2 1-oz. squares unsweetened chocolate
½ cup butter or margarine
1 cup sugar
2 eggs

1 teaspoon vanilla
½ cup sifted enriched flour
½ cup walnuts

Preheat oven to 325°. Melt chocolate over hot water. Thoroughly cream butter and sugar. Add eggs and beat well. Blend in melted chocolate, vanilla, and flour. Mix nuts into batter or sprinkle them over top of batter after it is poured into pan. Bake in greased 8 × 8 × 2-inch pan for 35 minutes. Frost with Fudge Frosting.

FUDGE FROSTING

1 stick butter
3 tablespoons cocoa
6 tablespoons milk

1 box confectioner's sugar
½ cup chopped walnuts
1 teaspoon vanilla

Do not cook; just mix well and pour over hot cake in pan.

FRANCES' LEMON SOURS

¾ cup flour
1 stick butter

½ cup brown sugar

Mix flour and butter; then cream in brown sugar. Grease 8 × 8-inch pan and pour mixture in. Bake 10 minutes at 300°. Let cool.

2 eggs
1 cup brown sugar
1 cup coconut
½ cup pecans

½ teaspoon baking powder
Pinch salt
½ teaspoon vanilla

Mix and spread on top of first mixture. Cook 15 to 20 minutes at 300°.

1 cup powdered sugar

juice of one lemon

Mix and pour over cake while it is still hot. Leave in pan to cool. Cut in squares and serve.

BROWN SUGAR MERINGUE COOKIES

2 egg whites
4 tablespoons brown sugar

½ teaspoon vanilla

Beat egg whites at high speed. Gradually add sugar and vanilla. Beat until the mixture stands in stiff peaks. Make sure it is beaten enough, but stop when stiff-peak stage is reached.

Cover cookie sheet with white shelf-lining paper. Drop cookies with demitasse spoon. Bake for 60-70 minutes at 225°.

FRENCH CREAM DESSERT

½ pound vanilla wafers
½ cup soft butter
1 cup confectioner's sugar

2 eggs
1 cup heavy cream
1 cup drained crushed pineapple

Roll wafers and put half in bottom of a buttered pan. Cream butter. Add sugar and beat well. Add eggs and mix well. Spread over crumbs. Whip cream and fold in nuts and pineapple. Spread over first two layers. Top with remaining crumbs. Refrigerate 24 hours. Makes 6 servings. (Frozen whipped topping may be substituted for whipped cream.)

PECAN PIE OR TARTS

1 cup sugar
1 cup white corn syrup
3 eggs, well beaten

1 cup pecan pieces
½ tablespoon flour
1 teaspoon orange extract

Mix and bake in unbaked pie shell or tart shells at 350° until done—about 1 hour.

RASPBERRY VELVET PIE

1 10-oz. package frozen raspberries, thawed
1 3-oz. package raspberry gelatin
1 cup boiling water

¼ pound marshmallows
1 cup heavy cream, whipped
Crumb crust

Drain berries, reserving syrup. Add enough water to syrup to make 1 cup. Dissolve gelatin in boiling water. Add marshmallows; stir till partially melted. Add reserved syrup; chill till partially set. Beat until fluffy and peaks form. Fold in berries and whipped cream. Pour into crumb crust and chill until set. Center with additional whipped cream and raspberries.

DESSERT RICE

2 cups cooked rice (not Minute Rice)
1 cup crushed pineapple

1 cup miniature marshmallows (pastel-
     colored great)
½ cup sugar

Mix rice, drained pineapple, marshmallows, and sugar. Just before serving, fold in whipped cream. (Frozen whipped topping can be used if desired.)

CARAMEL DUMPLINGS

1½ cups + 3 tablespoons sugar
⅛ teaspoon + ¼ teaspoon salt
1½ cups flour
½ cup chopped walnuts

5 tablespoons butter
2 cups hot water
2½ tablespoons baking powder
¾ cup milk

Heat ½ cup sugar in heavy skillet until it melts to golden brown syrup. Add 2 tablespoons butter, ⅛ teaspoon salt, and 1 cup sugar. Add hot water very gradually while stirring constantly. Bring to a boil and cook until sugar is dissolved (about 10 minutes). Stir frequently. Meanwhile, sift together flour, baking powder, remaining 3 tablespoons sugar, and salt. Mix in remaining 3 tablespoons butter until mixture is like coarse corn meal. Add walnuts; stir in milk all at once, mixing only enough to moisten flour. Drop by tablespoonfuls into gently boiling caramel sauce. Cook covered for 12-15 minutes. Serve hot with sauce.

EASY CARAMEL PIE

1 can sweetened condensed milk
1 pie shell, baked

Frozen whipped topping

Put milk, unopened, in a large saucepan. Cover can with water and bring to boil. Let simmer for 2½ to 3 hours. Remove from hot water and let it cool for 15-20 minutes; then open can and spread caramelized milk over baked pie shell. Chill and serve with whipped topping.

HELEN'S BLUEBERRY BANANA PIE

1 can wild blueberries	1 12-oz. carton frozen dessert topping
1 cup sugar	2 bananas
1 9-oz. package cream cheese	1 baked pie shell

Slice bananas and line crust with slices. Mix cheese, sugar, and topping. Spread over banana-covered shell. Drain blueberries thoroughly and spread over top of cheese mixture. (One can of berries makes enough for 2 pies. Be sure to get *wild* blueberries.)

LEMON PUDDING DELUXE

1 can sweetened condensed milk	2 cups sour cream
⅓ cup lemon juice	1⅓ cups (3½-oz.) flaked coconut
1 tablespoon grated lemon rind	1 cup heavy cream, whipped

In large-size bowl, blend sweetened condensed milk, lemon juice, and rind. Fold in sour cream and coconut. Spoon into individual parfait glasses or dessert dishes. Refrigerate until set. Garnish with whipped cream. Makes 8 half-cup servings.

ANGEL MIST

2 envelopes unflavored gelatin	½ cup sugar
3 cups milk	1 cup heavy cream, whipped, or 2 cups
4 eggs, separated	whipped topping
½ cup mint jelly	1 10-inch angel food cake, torn into
¾ teaspoon mint extract	small pieces
½ teaspoon green food coloring	Magic Chocolate Sauce (see page 103)

Sprinkle gelatin over milk in saucepan. Beat egg yolks until light and lemon colored and stir into milk. Stir over low heat until gelatin dissolves (about 5 minutes). Stir in jelly until melted. Remove from heat and stir in mint extract and coloring. Chill, stirring occasionally, until mixture mounds slightly when dropped from a spoon. Beat egg whites in large bowl until soft peaks form. Gradually add sugar and beat until stiff, but not dry. Fold whipped cream or topping into gelatin mixture; then fold in pieces of cake and meringue. Turn into 12-cup Bundt pan. Chill 4 hours, until firm (or overnight). Unmold and serve with chocolate sauce.

CREAM WAFER COOKIES

2 cups flour	⅓ cup cream
1 cup butter, soft	

Mix dough well and divide into thirds and chill. Roll 1 part at a time ⅛ inch thick and cut with 1½-inch cutter. Coat both sides of cookies with sugar and prick four times with fork. Bake at 375° for 7-9 minutes. Note: Keep remaining dough in refrigerator until ready to slice.

Filling:

¾ cup confectioner's sugar	1 egg yolk
¼ cup butter, soft	1 teaspoon vanilla

Blend together and use between two cookies. Filling may be tinted with food color if desired. Makes about 5 dozen double cookies.

FIG PRESERVES CAKE

Sift together:

2 cups plain flour	1 teaspoon cinnamon
1½ cups sugar	1 teaspoon nutmeg
1 teaspoon soda	½ teaspoon cloves

Add:

1 cup salad oil	1 cup fig preserves
3 eggs	1 teaspoon vanilla
1 cup buttermilk	

Cook in 8 × 13-inch greased pan for 45 minutes at 325°. Make holes in cake and pour topping over:

1 cup sugar	1 teaspoon corn syrup
1 stick butter	½ cup buttermilk
1 teaspoon vanilla	

Boil for three minutes.

HELEN'S JAM CAKE

1½ cups butter	1½ teaspoons soda
3 cups sugar	1½ teaspoons vanilla
1½ cups jam (strawberry, blackberry, or raspberry)	3¾ cups plain flour (measure before sifting)
1½ cups raisins	6 whole eggs
1½ cups buttermilk	1½ cups coconut

Makes 4 layers. Bake at 350° about 30 minutes.

Filling:

1 cup milk	1 tablespoon flour
1½ cups sugar	2 eggs

Cook until thick; then add:

1 cup nuts	1 cup raisins
1 cup coconut	1 teaspoon vanilla

Frosting:

2 sticks margarine	3 cups sugar

Brown sugar in margarine until light brown. Stir in 1½ cups milk and cook until soft ball stage. Add 1 teaspoon vanilla and beat until spreading consistency.

ORANGE MELTAWAYS

Cream 1½ sticks butter with ½ cup confectioner's sugar. Sift together 1 cup flour and ½ cup cornstarch and stir into butter mixture. Add 4 teaspoons grated orange rind and 1 teaspoon vanilla. Chill, covered, for 1 hour. Shape into 10-inch roll. Wrap in waxed paper and foil and place in freezer for 2 hours. Roll in granulated sugar and cut into ¼-inch slices. Arrange 2 inches apart on a buttered cookie sheet and bake at 375° for 10 minutes. Makes 40 cookies.

DOUBLE GOOD BANANA CAKE

3 cups all-purpose flour
2 cups sugar
1 teaspoon salt
1 teaspoon baking powder
1 teaspoon soda
1 package (4-serving size) banana cream pudding
    and pie filling mix

1½ cups sliced ripe bananas
1 cup butter, softened
⅓ cup milk
2 teaspoons vanilla
4 eggs

Glaze:

1½ cups confectioner's sugar
2 tablespoons butter, softened

½ teaspoon vanilla
1 to 2 tablespoons milk

Preheat oven to 325°. Generously grease and flour 12-cup Bundt pan. Lightly spoon flour into measuring cup; level off. In large bowl, blend all ingredients (except those for glaze) and beat 3 minutes at medium speed. Pour into prepared pan. Bake 60 to 75 minutes, or until toothpick inserted in center comes out clean. Cool in pan 15 minutes; then turn out on serving plate. Cool. In small bowl, blend glaze ingredients until smooth and spoon over cake.

DEVIL'S FOOD CUPCAKES

1 package devil's food cake mix
8 oz. package cream cheese
⅓ cup sugar

1 egg
6 oz. package chocolate morsels

Prepare cake mix according to package directions. Place paper liners in muffin tins, and spoon batter into cups, filling them ⅔ full.

Mix cream cheese, sugar and eggs, creaming well. Stir in chocolate morsels. Spoon 1½ teaspoons of cheese mixture into center of each muffin cup. Bake at 350° for 25 minutes. Cool for 10 minutes before removing from pan; then cool completely before removing paper. Makes about 30 cupcakes.

MAGIC CHOCOLATE SAUCE

1 can sweetened condensed milk
2 1-oz. squares unsweetened chocolate

½ to 1 cup hot water
½ teaspoon vanilla extract

In top of double boiler, combine milk and chocolate. Cook over hot water; stir until thickened. Remove from heat. Slowly stir in hot water until sauce is of desired thickness. Stir in vanilla. Serve hot or chilled on vanilla ice cream.

BAKED CUSTARD

⅔ cup sweetened condensed milk
2 cups hot water
3 eggs, slightly beaten

½ teaspoon salt
1 teaspoon vanilla
Nutmeg

Combine milk and water. Gradually stir in eggs, salt, and vanilla. Pour into a 1-quart shallow 7 × 7 × 2-inch baking dish. Sprinkle with nutmeg. Bake 40-50 minutes (or until knife inserted near center comes out clean) at 325°. Cool at room temperature.

COCONUT CUSTARD PIE

1 unbaked 9-inch pastry shell
⅔ cup sweetened condensed milk
2 cups hot water
½ teaspoon salt

½ teaspoon vanilla
3 eggs
1 cup flaked coconut

Blend condensed milk, water, salt, and vanilla. Beat eggs until just blended. Stir into condensed milk. Add coconut. Pour into shell. Bake at 425° ten minutes, then reduce heat to 300°. Bake 20-25 minutes or until knife inserted in center comes out clean. Cool at room temperature; then refrigerate.

KITTY'S NO-FAIL PIE CRUST

Mix 3 cups flour and 1 teaspoon salt. Cut in 1½ cups shortening. In a small bowl, mix 1 egg, slightly beaten, 1 teaspoon vinegar, and 5 tablespoons ice water. Work liquids into flour and shortening mixture. Divide into at least three parts and roll out crust. The balls will keep wrapped in foil in refrigerator a week or more. Makes 3 crusts.

PEAR PECAN DESSERT

½ cup butter
⅓ cup sugar
¼ teaspoon vanilla

¾ cup flour
⅔ cup walnuts, chopped

Cream butter and sugar; blend in vanilla; add flour; mix; add walnuts. Spread and press onto bottom of greased pan. Bake at 350 degrees about 20 minutes or until slightly brown in a 8 × 8 pan.

Filling:

8 oz. cream cheese
¼ cup sugar

½ teaspoon vanilla
1 egg

Blend cheese and sugar. Add egg and vanilla. Pour over cooled crust. Refrigerate until set (approximately 1 to 2 hours).

Topping:

1 large can pears, drained and cut into chunks, to
   be placed on top of filling

1 teaspoon sugar
½ teaspoon cinnamon

Mix and sprinkle the sugar and cinnamon over the pears. Bake everything at 325 degrees for 25 minutes. Note: for 9 × 13 × 2 pan: Crust needs to be doubled, the filling tripled, and the topping doubled.

BUTTERMILK PIE

12 eggs, beaten
7 cups sugar
2 sticks *butter*, melted

6 tablespoons flour (heaping)
6 teaspoons vanilla extract
3 cups buttermilk

Mix all ingredients together, in order listed. Pour into unbaked pie shells (for smaller 8-9″ shells, fill to edge of crust; for larger shells 10″, fill ½ to ⅔ to edge of crust). Bake at 325 degrees for 40 minutes. Note: 300 degrees for 30-35 minutes for a convection oven.

RAISIN-NUT PIE

2 eggs
1½ sticks butter or margarine
1 cup sugar
1 tablespoon lemon juice

1 cup white raisins
1½ teaspoons vanilla
¾ cup nuts

Beat eggs. Stir in butter, salt, sugar, lemon juice, and raisins. Bring to a full boil, stirring constantly. Boil 1 minute. Remove from heat and pour into baked pie shell. Refrigerate overnight and serve with whipped cream.

PETIT FOURS

Make your favorite white sheet cake. Cut into diamond-shaped pieces and ice with Deluxe Cream Cheese Frosting (page 113), tinted in colors to match your color scheme. If chocolate frosting is desired for some of the cake, use Chocolate Fudge Frosting (page 99). Rosy Chiffon Glaze (page 94) may also be used.

Petit fours may be decorated if you wish. Use a contrasting color of frosting for decorating.

JUDY'S BROWN SUGAR POUND CAKE

1 stick butter
1 cup vegetable shortening
3 cups flour
5 eggs
1 box brown sugar
1 cup plain sugar

1 tablespoon baking powder
1 cup milk
1 cup nuts
1 cup frozen coconut
1 teaspoon vanilla

Mix well; start in cold oven. Bake at 275° for two hours.

Glaze:
1 stick butter
¼ cup evaporated milk

1 cup brown sugar

Melt and pour over cake while hot.

RAINBOW PIES

Crust:
10 cups Graham crackers
1½ cups sugar

1 pound melted margarine

Filling:
8 cups hot pineapple juice
1½ pounds lemon gelatin
½ package lime gelatin

½ package strawberry gelatin
14 oz. sugar
3 quarts whipped topping

Mix and press the Graham cracker crust into pans and bake at 400° until done. Make the lime and the strawberry gelatins in separate pans the day ahead. Cut into small cubes. Mix hot pineapple juice and lemon gelatin and let set until like egg whites. Fold in 3 quarts whipped topping and gelatin cubes. Pour into crusts and top with crumbs. Chill. Serve with whipped topping. Makes 10 pies of 9-inch size.

PEACH COBBLER

1 #3 can sliced peaches
1 yellow cake mix

3 sticks butter or margarine
Almond flavoring

Place peaches in a 9 × 13 pan. Pour in 1 teaspoon almond extract and mix with juice. Pour cake mix evenly over peaches. Melt butter and drizzle evenly over cake mix. Bake at 350° until it browns on top.

APRICOT SOUR CREAM PIE

1 quart canned apricot halves
1½-pound package apricot-flavored gelatin
¼ cup sugar

3 quarts hot water
2 quarts sour cream
6 baked 9-inch pie shells (Graham cracker crumb)

Drain apricots, reserving syrup. Add water to syrup to make required amount of liquid. Dice the apricots. Dissolve the gelatin and sugar in hot water. Chill until slightly thickened. Blend in sour cream; stir in apricots. Pour into pie shells, allowing 1 qt. filling for each. Chill until set. Garnish with prepared whipped topping and additional apricots, sliced, if desired. (Plain or vanilla yogurt may be substituted for the sour cream.) Makes 6 pies of 9-inch size.

HANNAH'S CHOCOLATE FUDGE PIE

1 stick margarine
3 tablespoons cocoa
1 cup sugar

¼ cup flour
2 eggs
1 teaspoon vanilla

Melt margarine and cocoa together. Beat together with remaining ingredients and pour into unbaked pie shells. Bake 35 to 40 minutes at 325°.

COCONUT PECAN PIE

3 eggs, beaten until thick
1 cup sugar
1 cup white Karo syrup

1 teaspoon vanilla extract
½ cup coconut
1 cup + 1 tablespoon Texas pecans

Combine all ingredients. Place in an unbaked pie shell and bake at 350 degrees for 20 minutes; then cut back to 325 degrees til pie sets.

CHEESE CAKE

6¾ cups Graham cracker crumbs
¾ cup sugar
1½ cups softened butter or margarine
3 pounds cream cheese
2½ quarts chilled milk

3 tablespoons grated lemon rind
2 pounds instant vanilla pudding
4 tablespoons plain gelatin
½ cup cold water

Prepare crumb shells. Combine crumbs, sugar, and butter and mix well. Set aside ½ cup to sprinkle on top of cake. Press remainder into bottoms of four ½″ spring form cake pans or bottoms and sides of six 9-inch pie pans. Bake in moderate oven about five minutes and then cool. Soften cream cheese in mixer, using paddle, and blend in small amount of chilled milk. Scrape bowl. Then add rest of milk gradually, blending thoroughly. Add lemon rind. Insert whip. Add pie filling powder and whip at a low speed until powder is dampened (about 15 seconds). Then whip at medium speed until smooth (1 to 2 minutes.) Soften plain gelatin in cold water. Dissolve in pan of hot water. Add to mixture. Pour at once into crumb-lined pans. Sprinkle with reserved crumbs. Chill until firm. Makes 50 servings.

CHEESE CUSTARD TARTS

2 pounds cream cheese, softened
3 quarts milk
½ cup sugar
1 18-oz. package custard mix

1 tablespoon grated lemon rind
48 3-inch tart shells
Canned blueberry, peach, or cherry pie
    filling—as needed

Blend cream cheese with a small amount of the milk in saucepot or steam-jacketed kettle until smooth. Blend in remaining milk and the sugar and heat. Add custard mix to hot milk mixture. Stir well with a wire whip until well blended. Add lemon rind and pour at once into tart shells, allowing ⅓ cup for each. Let cool 15 minutes. Chill until set, about 4 hours. Top with pie filling. Makes 1 gallon—enough for 48 tarts of 3-inch size.

PEANUT BUTTER CHOCOLATE PUDDING

1 30-oz. box rice pudding mix
5 quarts milk
1½ pounds chocolate-flavored baking chips

8 oz. miniature marshmallows
2 cups creamy or chunky peanut butter

Add pudding mix to milk in saucepan. Cook, stirring often, until mixture comes to a full boil. (Mixture will be thin; it thickens as it cools.) Remove from heat; stir in chips, marshmallows, and peanut butter, blending until smooth. Pour into a shallow pan. Cool 15 minutes, stirring occasionally to prevent formation of skin. Stir well; then cover surface with plastic wrap. Serve warm or chilled. Garnish with prepared whipped topping and chocolate sprinkles or chopped peanuts. Makes 1¾ gallons—56 portions of ½ cup each.

COCOA SPONGE ROLL

2¾ cups sifted cake flour
1⅓ cups cocoa
1 cup sugar
1 tablespoon baking powder
1 teaspoon salt

20 eggs
3½ cups sugar
2 tablespoons vanilla
Confectioner's sugar as needed

Generously grease flour 15 × 10-inch jelly roll pans. Line with wax paper, allowing paper to extend about 2 inches at each end; grease the paper. Sift flour with cocoa, sugar, baking powder, and salt. Whip eggs at high speed until thick and light in color. Gradually add sugar, beating thoroughly after each addition. At low speed, gradually fold in flour mixture; blend in vanilla. Pour into pans, allowing about 1¼ pound per pan. Bake at 350° for 20 to 25 minutes or until cakes spring back when lightly pressed. Cool in pans 3 to 5 minutes; then turn onto cloths which have been sprinkled lightly with confectioner's sugar. Quickly remove paper and trim off crisp edges. Roll up cakes in cloth. Cool on racks. Makes 4 cake rolls.

WHIPPED ANGEL FOOD PIE

2-4 oz. lemon gelatin
6 cups sugar
9 cups hot water

4 cups hot lemon juice
3 tablespoons lemon rind
3 gallons whipped topping

Crusts:

12 cups Graham cracker crumbs
2 cups sugar

1¼ pounds margarine, melted

Dissolve gelatin and sugar in hot water. Add lemon juice. Chill until like egg whites. Add lemon rind. Fold in whipped topping. Pour in pie shells. Garnish with mint leaves and crumbs. Chill. Makes 12 pies.

COCONUT CLOUD

1 cup Graham cracker crumbs
3 tablespoons sugar
3 tablespoons butter or margarine, melted
2 ½-oz. envelopes whipped topping mix
¾ cup milk

1 3¾-oz. package vanilla instant pudding
 and pie filling mix
½ teaspoon vanilla extract
1 cup commercial sour cream
1 cup flaked coconut, divided

Combine Graham cracker crumbs, sugar, and butter; mix well, and press onto bottom of an 8-inch spring-form pan. Bake at 350° for 8 minutes; cool completely.

Prepare whipped topping mix according to package directions. Set aside.

Combine milk, pudding mix, and vanilla; beat at medium speed of electric mixer 1 minute. Add sour cream, mixing well. Fold in half of prepared whipped topping and ¾ cup coconut.

Spoon filling over prepared crust. Top with remaining whipped topping, and sprinkle with ¼ cup coconut. Chill overnight. Makes 6 to 8 servings.

LEMON CAKE ROLL

4 eggs, separated
¼ cup sugar
1 teaspoon lemon extract
1 tablespoon vegetable oil
½ cup sugar
⅔ cup sifted cake flour
1 teaspoon baking powder

¼ teaspoon salt
Powdered sugar
Creamy Lemon Filling
½ cup flaked coconut
½ teaspoon water
1 to 2 drops yellow food coloring

Beat egg yolks until light and lemon colored; gradually add ¼ cup sugar, beating constantly. Stir in lemon extract and vegetable oil; set aside.

Beat egg whites until foamy; gradually add ½ cup sugar, beating until stiff but not dry. Fold yolk mixture into whites. Combine flour, baking powder, and salt; fold into egg mixture.

Grease a 15 × 10 × 1-inch jelly roll pan, and line with waxed paper; grease and flour waxed paper. Spread butter evenly in pan. Bake at 375° for 10 to 12 minutes.

Sift powdered sugar in a 15 × 10-inch rectangle on a linen towel. When cake is done, immediately loosen from sides of pan and turn out on sugar. Peel off waxed paper. Starting at narrow end, roll up cake and towel together; cook on a wire rack, seam side down.

Unroll cake; spread with half of Creamy Lemon Filling, and reroll. Place on serving plate, seam side down; spread remaining filling on all sides.

Combine coconut, water, and food coloring in a plastic bag; close securely, and shake well. Sprinkle colored coconut over cake roll. Refrigerate for 1 to 2 hours before serving. Makes 8 to 10 servings.

CREAMY LEMON FILLING

1 14-oz. can sweetened condensed milk
⅓ cup lemon juice
1 to 2 teaspoons grated lemon rind

5 drops yellow food coloring
1 4-oz. carton frozen whipped topping,
    thawed

Combine sweetened condensed milk, lemon juice, lemon rind, and food coloring; mix well. Fold in whipped topping. Makes about 3 cups.

CHOCOLATE CREAM CHEESE PIE

1½ cups finely crushed chocolate wafers
⅓ cup margarine, melted
1 8-oz. package cream cheese, softened
¼ cup sugar
1 teaspoon vanilla extract
2 egg yolks
1 6-oz. package semi-sweet chocolate morsels, melted

2 egg whites (at room temperature)
¼ cup sugar
1 cup thawed frozen whipped topping
¾ cup chopped pecans
Whipped topping (optional)
Chocolate curls (optional)

Combine crushed wafers and margarine, stirring well. Press mixture into a 9-inch pie pan, and bake at 325° for 10 minutes. Cool completely.

Combine cream cheese, ¼ cup sugar, and vanilla; beat until smooth and creamy. Add egg yolks, beating until smooth. Stir in melted chocolate.

Beat egg whites until foamy; gradually add ¼ cup sugar, beating until stiff peaks form. Fold into chocolate mixture.

Gently fold 1 cup whipped topping and pecans into chocolate mixture; pour into prepared crust. Freeze pie at least 3 hours. Serve with a dollop of whipped topping, and garnish with chocolate curls, if desired. Makes one 9-inch pie.

CREOLE PEACH DIP

2 cups puréed fresh peaches
½ cup sugar
1 teaspoon lemon juice

Dash of salt
2 cups frozen whipped topping, thawed

Combine peaches, sugar, lemon juice, and salt; stir well. Fold in whipped topping. Chill until serving time. Serve with thin wafers or lightly flavored cookies. Makes about 4 cups.

ICE CREAM DELIGHT

1 cup saltine cracker crumbs
1 cup Graham cracker crumbs
½ cup melted butter or margarine
1 quart butter-pecan ice cream, softened
2 3¾-oz. packages instant vanilla pudding and pie
    filling mix

2 cups milk
1 12-oz. carton frozen whipped topping,
    thawed
3 1³⁄₁₆-oz. chocolate-covered toffee bars,
    chopped

Combine cracker crumbs and butter, stirring well; press into a 13 × 9 × 2-inch baking pan. Bake at 350° for 5 to 8 minutes. Allow to cool.

Combine ice cream, pudding mix, and milk; beat at low speed of electric mixer 2 minutes. Pour ice cream mixture over crust, and chill until set.

Spread whipped topping over ice cream, and sprinkle with candy. Makes 12 to 15 servings.

STRAWBERRY TARTS

¼ cup sugar
1 tablespoon all-purpose flour
Dash of salt
½ cup milk
1 egg, well beaten
¼ teaspoon vanilla extract

⅓ cup whipping cream, whipped
8 3-inch baked tart shells
1 pint fresh strawberries, washed and
    hulled
Currant jelly

Combine sugar, flour, and salt in top of a double boiler; stir in milk. Cook mixture over boiling water, stirring constantly, until thickened.

Stir some of hot mixture into egg. Stir egg mixture into remaining hot mixture. Cook over boiling water, stirring constantly, until thickened. Remove from heat, and add vanilla. Set aside to cool.

Fold cooled custard into whipped cream. Spoon into tart shells, filling half full. Arrange 4 to 5 strawberries over filling. Spread 1 teaspoon jelly on each tart, filling in between strawberries. Chill well before serving. Makes 8 servings.

CHOCOLATE MINT CUPS

2 1-oz. squares unsweetened chocolate, melted
1 cup butter, softened
2 cups powdered sugar
4 eggs

2 teaspoons vanilla extract
1 teaspoon peppermint extract
12 vanilla wafers, finely crushed
¼ cup finely chopped pecans

Melt chocolate over low heat, stirring constantly. Set chocolate aside to cool.

Combine butter and sugar, creaming until light and fluffy. Add eggs, one at a time, beating well after each addition. Add chocolate and flavorings; mix well.

Combine vanilla wafer crumbs and pecans; stir well. Sprinkle half of crumb mixture into 12 ungreased muffin cups.

Spoon chocolate mixture over crumb mixture, and top with remaining crumb mixture. Cover and freeze until firm.

To serve, run a knife around edge of each muffin cup; gently lift out dessert with knife. Makes 12 servings.

OATMEAL COOKIES

1 cup all-purpose flour
½ teaspoon soda
½ teaspoon salt
1 teaspoon ground cinnamon
¼ teaspoon ground nutmeg
½ cup firmly packed brown sugar

¼ cup sugar
½ cup shortening
1 egg
2 tablespoons milk
2 cups quick-cooking oats, uncooked
1 cup raisins

Combine flour, soda, salt, and spices; set aside.

Combine sugar and shortening, creaming well; beat in egg and milk. Add flour mixture, mixing well. Stir in the oats and raisins.

Drop dough by heaping teaspoonfuls onto lightly greased cookie sheets. Bake at 375° for 10 to 12 minutes or until lightly browned. Cool slightly on cookie sheets; remove to wire racks to cool completely. Makes about 3½ dozen.

LEMON ICE CREAM PIE

1½ pints vanilla ice cream
3 eggs
½ cup sugar
½ teaspoon salt

¼ cup lemon juice
1 cup whipping cream, whipped
Grated lemon rind (optional)
Mint leaves (optional)

Cut ice cream into ½-inch slices, and arrange on bottom and sides of a lightly greased 9-inch pie pan. Let ice cream soften slightly; then smooth slices together with a spoon, forming a pie shell. Freeze 2½ hours or until firm.

Combine 1 egg and 2 egg yolks in a small, heavy saucepan; beat well. Stir in sugar, salt, and lemon juice. Cook over low heat, stirring constantly, until thickened. Set aside to cool. Fold mixture into whipped cream.

Beat 2 egg whites until stiff; fold into lemon mixture. Spoon filling into ice cream shell. Freeze until firm (about 5 hours). Let stand at room temperature 5 minutes before slicing. Garnish with grated lemon rind and mint leaves, if desired. Makes one 9-inch pie.

ORANGE NUT CAKE

½ cup butter or margarine, softened
¼ cup shortening
1½ cups sugar
3 eggs
2½ cups all-purpose flour
1½ teaspoons soda
¾ teaspoon salt

1½ cups buttermilk
1½ teaspoons vanilla extract
1 cup golden raisins, chopped
1 cup finely chopped pecans or walnuts
1 tablespoon grated orange rind
Orange Buttercream Frosting

Combine butter, shortening, and sugar; cream until light and fluffy. Add eggs, one at a time, beating well after each addition. Add flour, soda, salt, buttermilk, and vanilla; mix just until blended. Beat at high speed of electric mixer 3 minutes.

Stir raisins, pecans, and orange rind into batter; spoon into 3 greased and floured 8-inch cakepans. Bake at 350° for 30 to 35 minutes or until cake tests done. Cool 5 to 10 minutes in pans; remove from pans, and cool completely.

Spread Orange Buttercream Frosting between layers and on top and sides of cake. Makes one 8-inch layer cake.

ORANGE BUTTERCREAM FROSTING

1½ cups butter or margarine, softened
4½ cups powdered sugar

2 tablespoons orange juice
1 tablespoon grated orange rind

Combine butter and sugar, creaming until light and fluffy. Add orange juice; beat until spreading consistency. Stir in orange rind. Makes enough for one 3-layer cake.

BUTTER COOKIES

3 sticks butter
1 cup sugar
1 egg (don't beat)

1 teaspoon vanilla
4 cups flour

Cream butter and sugar. Add flour gradually. Add egg and vanilla. Roll in sticks on waxed paper. Chill or freeze. Cut thin and bake at 350 degrees for 10 minutes (or until light brown). Makes 75-90 cookies.

CARROT-LEMON SQUARES

1 cup melted margarine	1½ teaspoons vanilla extract
1¼ cups sugar	¾ teaspoon lemon extract
4 eggs	2¼ cups powdered sugar
1 cup cooked, mashed carrots	¼ cup water
2 cups all-purpose flour	1½ teaspoons lemon extract
1 teaspoon baking powder	

Combine margarine and sugar in a large mixing bowl; mix well. Add eggs, one at a time, beating well after each addition. Add carrots, flour, and baking powder; beat 1 minute. Stir in vanilla and ¾ teaspoon lemon extract. Spoon into a greased 15 × 10 × 1-inch jelly roll pan, spreading to edges. Bake at 350° for 25 minutes. Cool.

Combine powdered sugar, water, and 1½ teaspoons lemon extract; stir until smooth. Pour glaze over cooled cake. Let stand until glaze is firm. Cut into squares. Makes about 5 dozen (1½ inch squares).

PEACHES AND CREAM CAKE

1 18½-oz. package butter-flavored cake mix	2 cups whipping cream
1½ cups sugar	2-3 tablespoons powdered sugar
4 tablespoons cornstarch	1 cup commercial sour cream
4 cans chopped fresh peaches	Fresh sliced peaches
½ cup water	

Prepare cake according to package directions, using two 8-inch cakepans. Cool and split each layer.

Combine sugar and cornstarch in a saucepan. Add peaches and water; cook over medium heat, stirring constantly, until smooth and thickened. Cool mixture completely.

Combine whipping cream and powdered sugar in a medium mixing bowl; beat until stiff peaks form.

Spoon ⅓ of peach filling over split layer of cake; spread ⅓ cup sour cream over filling. Repeat procedure with remaining cake layers, peach filling, and sour cream, ending with remaining cake layer. Frost with sweetened whipping cream, and garnish with fresh peach slices. Makes one 8-inch cake.

PEACH DUMPLINGS

2-2½ cups all-purpose flour	Ground cinnamon
2 teaspoons baking powder	⅔ cup sugar
1 teaspoon salt	1½ cups water
¾ cup shortening	2 tablespoons butter or margarine
½ cup milk	¼ teaspoon ground cinnamon
4 medium peaches, peeled and halved	Dash of ground nutmeg
Sugar	Whipping cream

Combine flour, baking powder, and salt; cut in shortening with pastry blender until mixture resembles coarse meal. Gradually add milk, stirring to make a soft dough. Roll dough into a 14-inch square (¼-inch thickness) on a lightly floured surface; then cut dough into four 7-inch squares.

Place 2 peach halves on each square. Sprinkle each with 2 teaspoons sugar and ⅛ teaspoon cinnamon. Moisten edges of each dumpling with water; bring corners to center, pinching edges to seal.

Place dumplings 1 inch apart in a lightly greased shallow baking pan.

Combine remaining ingredients except whipping cream in a medium saucepan; place over low heat, stirring until butter melts and sugar dissolves. Pour syrup over dumplings. Bake at 425° for 40 to 45 minutes or until golden brown. Serve with cream. Makes 4 servings.

CREAM CHEESE CAKE

3 cups all-purpose flour
2 cups sugar
1 teaspoon soda
1 teaspoon salt
1 teaspoon ground cloves
3 eggs, beaten

1¼ cups vegetable oil
1 teaspoon almond extract
1 8-oz. can crushed pineapple, undrained
1 cup chopped toasted almonds
2 cups mashed banana
Cream Cheese Frosting

Combine first 5 ingredients in a large mixing bowl; add eggs and oil, stirring until dry ingredients are moistened. Do not beat. Stir in almond extract, pineapple, almonds, and banana.

Spoon batter into a greased and floured 10-inch tube pan. Bake at 300° for 1 hour and 15 minutes. Cool in pan 10 minutes; remove cake from pan, and cool completely.

Frost cake with Cream Cheese Frosting. Makes one 10-inch cake.

CREAM CHEESE FROSTING

½ cup butter or margarine, softened
1 8-oz. package cream cheese, softened
1 16-oz. package powdered sugar

1 tablespoon instant tea
⅛ teaspoon salt

Cream butter and cream cheese; gradually add sugar, tea, and salt, beating until light and fluffy. Makes enough for one 10-inch cake.

PINEAPPLE PUDDING

6 tablespoons butter or margarine
4½ cups sugar
9 tablespoons all-purpose flour
Pinch of salt
9 eggs, beaten
6 cups milk
¾ cup evaporated milk

3 8¼-oz. cans crushed pineapple, undrained
1 tablespoon vanilla extract
3 cups chopped pecans or walnuts
Vanilla wafers (about 12 dozen)
3 cups whipping cream, whipped

Melt butter in a heavy saucepan. Stir in sugar, flour, and salt. Add eggs and milk, stirring until blended. Cook over medium heat, stirring, until thickened. Remove from heat; stir in pineapple, vanilla, and pecans. Cool.

Line bottom and sides of a lightly greased casserole with vanilla wafers. Spoon in half of pudding. Top with a layer of vanilla wafers and remaining pudding. Arrange additional vanilla wafers around outside edge of pudding, and top with whipped cream.

PINEAPPLE UPSIDE-DOWN CAKE

3 tablespoons butter or margarine, melted
1 cup firmly packed brown sugar
1 15½-oz. can sliced pineapple, drained
½ cup shortening
1 cup sugar
2 eggs

1½ cups all-purpose flour
2 teaspoons baking powder
½ teaspoon salt
⅔ cup milk
1 teaspoon vanilla extract

Melt butter in a 10-inch cast-iron skillet. Spread brown sugar evenly over butter. Arrange pineapple on sugar.

Combine shortening and sugar, creaming until light and fluffy. Add eggs and mix well.

Stir in remaining ingredients; beat 2 minutes or until batter is smooth and fluffy. Spoon batter evenly over pineapple slices. Bake at 350° for 50 to 55 minutes or until cake tests done. Cool 5 minutes, and invert cake onto plate.

DEEP-DISH BLACKBERRY COBBLER

4 cups fresh blackberries or 2 (16-oz.) packages
   frozen blackberries, thawed
1 cup sugar
2 tablespoons all-purpose flour
2 tablespoons lemon juice

⅛ teaspoon salt
Triple-crust pastry (recipe follows)
1½ tablespoons butter or margarine,
   divided

Combine berries, sugar, flour, lemon juice, and salt; stir well.

Prepare pastry, and divide dough in half. Roll half of dough to ⅛-inch thickness to fit sides and bottom of a lightly greased 2-quart baking dish. Spoon half of berry mixture into pastry-lined dish; dot with half of butter.

Divide remaining dough in half. Roll one portion of dough into a rectangle; place over berries, making a few slits in pastry. Top with remaining berry mixture, and dot with remaining butter. Roll out remaining portion of dough to fit top of baking dish. Cover dish, and seal pastry edges. Make slits along top.

Bake at 450° for 10 minutes; reduce heat to 350° and bake 45 minutes longer or until bubbly and golden brown. Serve warm. Makes 6 servings.

TRIPLE-CRUST PASTRY

2 cups all-purpose flour
¾ teaspoon salt

⅔ cup shortening
3 tablespoons ice water

Combine flour and salt; cut in shortening until mixture resembles coarse crumbs. Sprinkle water over mixture, and stir with a fork; shape dough into a ball. Makes crust for 1 cobbler.

CHESS TARTS

3 whole eggs
1 stick butter
½ tablespoon vinegar

½ teaspoon vanilla
1 tablespoon corn meal
1½ cups sugar

Cream butter and sugar. Add eggs one at a time. Stir in vinegar, vanilla, and meal. Bake in unbaked tart shells for 45 minutes at 325 °. (Check them after 25 minutes.) Makes 12 tarts.

CRESCENTS

½ pound margarine
2 teaspoons vanilla
4 tablespoons heaping, powdered sugar

¾ cup chopped pecans
2 cups flour
Pinch of salt

Blend all ingredients. (If too stiff to handle, add 2 teaspoons water.) Take a small piece and make a roll. Turn at the end to make a crescent. Bake in slow oven (350°). Dust with powdered sugar.

PEACHY BLUEBERRY COBBLER

1 cup sugar
1 cup all-purpose flour
2 teaspoons baking powder
1 teaspoon salt
1 cup milk

½ cup butter or margarine, melted
3 medium peaches, peeled, sliced, and
    lightly sugared
⅔ cup fresh or frozen blueberries
Vanilla ice cream (optional)

Combine dry ingredients in a medium mixing bowl. Combine milk and butter; pour over dry ingredients, and mix until smooth. Pour into a greased 12 × 8 × 2-inch glass baking dish.

Spread peaches evenly over top of batter; sprinkle with blueberries. Bake at 350° for 50 minutes or until batter rises through the fruit and top is golden brown. Serve cobbler warm and topped with vanilla ice cream, if desired. Makes 8 to 10 servings.

Note: Two (10-oz.) packages frozen peaches, thawed and drained, may be substituted for fresh peaches.

BUTTERSCOTCH BARS

3 pounds sifted flour
1 oz. salt
1 oz. baking powder
2 pounds shortening
3 pounds brown sugar, packed

4 teaspoons vanilla
1 quart milk
4½ quarts rolled oats
2 cups dry, shredded coconut

Sift together flour, salt, and baking powder into mixer bowl. Add shortening, sugar, vanilla, and the milk. Mix until smooth, about 2 minutes on low speed. Add, and mix only until blended. Spread ½ inch thick on 2 greased baking sheets and bake at 350° for 25 to 30 minutes. Cut into bars while warm; cool and remove from pan. Sprinkle with powdered sugar. Note: Shortening must be at room temperature in order to blend easily with other ingredients. Makes 100 servings in two 16 × 25 sheet pans.

CHERRY TARTS

1 48-oz. package cream cheese
2¼ cups sugar
6 eggs
3 teaspoons vanilla

3 tablespoons lemon extract
Vanilla wafers
3 cans cherry pie filling

Cream sugar into cream cheese. Add eggs, vanilla, and lemon extract. Place a vanilla wafer in the bottom of a paper baking cup in muffin tin. Pour mixture into baking cups, filling them ½ to ⅔ full. Bake at 375° for 25 minutes or until starting to brown. (They will be muffin shaped when taken from the oven, but will sink to a tart shell shape as they cool.) Remove paper baking cups when cool. Top with cherry pie filling. Use about 3 cherries on each tart. Refrigerate. Makes 60.

CHOCOLATE CHIP PIE

1 stick margarine, melted
4 eggs, beaten
1 cup sugar
1 cup white Karo

1 cup chopped pecans
1 small package chocolate chips (6 oz.)
2 unbaked pie shells

Divide nuts and chips in bottom of 2 unbaked pie shells. Pour mixture of butter, sugar, eggs, and Karo over nuts and chips. Bake 30 to 40 minutes at 350 degrees.

LOUISIANA YAM CHEESE CAKE

1⅔ cups Graham cracker crumbs
¼ cup melted butter or margarine
1½ tablespoons unflavored gelatin
6 tablespoons cold water
3 eggs, separated
¾ cup sugar
½ teaspoon salt

⅓ cup milk
8 oz. cream cheese, softened
6 oz. cream cheese, softened
2 cups Louisiana Yams, cooked, peeled,
    and mashed
1 cup heavy cream, whipped

Reserve ½ cup crumbs for topping. Combine remaining crumbs and butter or margarine; mix well. Press crumb mixture over bottom of 8-inch spring-form pan. Soften gelatin in water. Blend egg yolks, ½ cup sugar, salt, and milk. Cook over low heat, stirring constantly, until thickened. Add softened gelatin and stir until gelatin dissolves. Add cheese and yams. Beat until well blended. Chill until slightly thickened. Beat egg whites until foamy. Gradually add remaining ¼ cup sugar, beating constantly, until stiff and glossy. Fold egg whites and cream into yam mixture. Turn into crumb-lined pan. Top with reserve crumbs. Chill until firm.

PEANUT BUTTER COOKIES

1 cup shortening
1 cup sugar
1 cup brown sugar
2 eggs
1 teaspoon vanilla

1 cup chunky peanut butter
3 cups flour
¼ teaspoon soda
½ teaspoon salt
1 cup chocolate chips (optional)

Cream shortening, sugars, eggs, vanilla. Beat well. Stir in peanut butter. Sift flour, salt, and soda. Stir into creamed mixture. Add chips. Form small balls. Bake on ungreased cookie sheet for 10 minutes at 350°. Makes 6 dozen.

SUGAR COOKIES

⅔ cup shortening
1 egg
¾ cup sugar
1 teaspoon vanilla
1½ cups flour

1½ teaspoons baking powder
½ cup nuts
4 teaspoons milk
¼ teaspoon salt

Soften shortening; blend in sugar. Add eggs. Beat until fluffy. Add vanilla. Sift flour, baking powder, and salt. Add milk to shortening and egg. Add flour and mix. Drop on greased cookie sheet. Bake for 12 minutes at 375°.

COCONUT SHEET CAKE

1 Duncan Hines butter cake mix (cook by directions
    on box)
2 cups milk

1 cup sugar
1 package (small) frozen fresh coconut

Mix milk, sugar, and coconut. Bring to a boil. Punch holes (lots of them) in cake as soon as you take it out of the oven. Pour above mixture over cake and let it soak into the cake. (Use a meat fork.) When cake cools, spread 1 8-ounce package of Cool Whip over cake and sprinkle with another package of fresh frozen coconut over Cool Whip. Refrigerate until cold. Keep in refrigerator.

PEANUT-CHOCOLATE DESSERT

½ cup butter or margarine, softened
1 cup all-purpose flour
⅔ cup finely chopped dry roasted peanuts
1 8-oz. package cream cheese, softened
⅓ cup powdered sugar
1 12-oz. carton frozen whipped topping, thawed
    and divided

1 3¾-oz. package vanilla instant pudding
    and pie filling mix
2¾ cups milk
1 1.2-oz. milk chocolate candy bar,
    shaved
⅓ cup chopped dry roasted peanuts

Cut butter into flour until mixture resembles coarse meal; stir ⅔ cup peanuts into flour mixture. Press peanut mixture into a 13 × 9 × 2-inch baking pan. Bake at 350° for 20 minutes; cool completely.

Combine cream cheese, peanut butter, and powdered sugar; beat until fluffy. Stir 1 cup whipped topping into cream cheese mixture. Spread over crust; chill.

Combine pudding mix and milk; beat 2 minutes at medium speed of electric mixer. Spread pudding over cream cheese layer. Spread remaining whipped topping over pudding layer. Sprinkle the top with shaved chocolate and ⅓ cup chopped peanuts. Store in refrigerator. Makes about 15 servings.

NO-BAKE ORANGE ROLLS

2 4-pound boxes vanilla wafers, crushed
12 cups grated coconut

12 cups confectioner's sugar (4 lbs.)
8 cups frozen orange juice concentrate

Mix wafers, coconut, sugar. Add thawed orange juice. Form into 1-inch balls. Roll balls in additional confectioner's sugar. Makes 475 balls.

COCONUT POUND CAKE

2½ cups sugar
1½ cups Crisco
5 eggs
3 cups flour, all-purpose
1 teaspoon baking powder

¼ teaspoon salt
1 cup milk
1 can angel flake
2 teaspoons coconut flavoring

Cream together (by hand) sugar and Crisco. Add eggs one at a time and beat 2 minutes after each addition. Sift together flour, baking powder, and salt. Alternately add milk and flour mixture to egg mixture. Add coconut and flavoring. Bake in medium-sized steam pan ⅔ full and balance in small loaf pan. Grease and flour pans and start cake in cold oven. Set temperature at 350° and bake 1 hour and 25 minutes. Freezes well.

ICE CREAM PIE

2 Graham cracker crusts, baked and chilled
    thoroughly
⅔ cup Pet milk

2 packages (6-oz.) chocolate chips
1 tablespoon grated orange rind

Heat Pet milk and add chocolate chips. Add orange rind. Pour a little over bottom of crust. Alternate globs of vanilla ice cream and orange sherbet. Use more vanilla than orange. Dribble layer of chocolate over this, then another layer of sherbet and ice cream. Top with dribbles of chocolate. Freeze and serve as needed. Serves 12.

LAYER PIE

First layer (in mixer):
1 cup flour
1 stick margarine, creamed

1 cup chopped pecans

Blend, press in bottom of dish. Bake at 350° until *light* brown (about 30 minutes). Allow to cool.

Second layer (in mixer):
1 cup confectioner's sugar

8-oz. package cream cheese, creamed

Stir in 1½ cups Cool Whip. Spread over first layer.

Third layer:
3 cups cold milk
1 box instant chocolate jello pudding

1 small box vanilla pudding

Mix and spread over second layer. Top with layer of cool whip. Shave Hershey bar on top. Cherries are optional.

FIG CAKE

2 cups flour
1 teaspoon salt
1 teaspoon soda
1½ cups sugar
1 cup oil

3 eggs
1 cup buttermilk
1 cup fig preserves
1 cup nuts
1½ teaspoons vanilla

Sift flour, salt, soda, and sugar. Add oil and eggs. Add buttermilk gradually. Add figs, nuts, vanilla. Pour in greased loaf pan. Bake at 325° for 45 minutes. Pour sauce over warm cake while in pan.

SAUCE

1 cup sugar
1 stick margarine
1 tablespoon corn syrup

1 teaspoon vanilla
½ cup buttermilk
½ teaspoon soda

Mix all ingredients and boil for 5 minutes.

CHOCO-MOUSSE CAKE

1 tablespoon unflavored gelatin
1 cup sugar
Pinch of salt
⅔ cup water
6 squares unsweetened chocolate
8 egg yolks, unbeaten

2 teaspoons vanilla extract
8 egg whites
1 cup heavy cream
1 cup finely chopped black walnuts
48 lady fingers, split

Combine in top of double boiler: gelatin, sugar, salt, water, and chocolate. Cook over hot (not boiling) water, stirring until chocolate is melted and gelatin is dissolved. Remove from heat and add egg yolks, one at a time, beating well after each addition. Cook over boiling water, stirring 2 minutes. Add vanilla and cool. Beat egg whites until stiff, but not dry; fold into chocolate mixture; refrigerate 15 minutes. Fold in whipped cream and nuts. Grease 4-quart spring-bottom pan; line bottom and sides with split lady fingers; add thin layer of chocolate mixture, then more lady fingers. Repeat until all used, ending with chocolate. Refrigerate 12 to 24 hours. To serve: Unmold and ice with 2 cups heavy cream, whipped; then drizzle chocolate syrup over top made from 1 package chip chocolates and 1 cup white Karo syrup, dissolved over hot water, then slightly cooled. Serves 16 to 20.

DATE BARS

3 eggs

1 cup white sugar

1 cup flour

1 teaspoon baking powder

¼ teaspoon salt

1 package cut dates

1 cup nuts

Beat egg yolks. Stir in sugar and cream well. Add flour, to which has been added baking powder and salt, then stiffly beaten egg whites. Slightly flour dates and nuts and add alternately. Put in greased and floured 12 × 8-inch pan. Bake at 350° for 25 minutes. Should be chewy in the middle. While hot, cut in narrow bars and sprinkle with powdered sugar. (If a pyrex pan is used, increase baking time to about 1 hour.)

PINEAPPLE FRAPPE

2 cups fresh pineapple (be sure it is ripe)

1 cup ice

6 mint leaves

Put in blender at high speed. Serve at once in well-chilled glasses. A good low-calorie dessert.

Beverages

EXTRA SPECIAL PUNCH

12 quarts Catawba grape juice

6 quarts Ice Cream Parlor Lemon Peel Sherbet

Allow sherbet to soften and pour grape juice over it. Serves about 100. Since this flavor of sherbet is not available at all times, you may substitute any lemon sherbet—or pineapple.

This punch is expensive but is extra special!

COFFEE FOR A CROWD
(When you don't have a coffeemaker)

Make a muslin bag large enough to hold twice as much coffee as you will be using. Put two gallons of water in a large kettle, and put one pound of regular ground coffee in the bag. When water boils, drop coffee bag in kettle, cover tightly, and turn heat on low. Simmer for 10-12 minutes, stirring coffee bag around occasionally. Do not allow it to boil. This will make about 40-50 servings.

APRICOT COFFEE PUNCH

1 cup chilled apricot nectar
1⅓ cups brewed coffee, chilled
½ pint coffee ice cream, softened

¾ cup milk
½ teaspoon almond extract

Combine all ingredients; beat with mixer until frothy and pour into punch bowl or pitcher. Will make about 8 punch-cup servings.

MOCHA PUNCH

6 cups cold water
1 cup instant coffee
1 cup chocolate syrup

4 cups milk
4 pints chocolate ice cream
2 teaspoons almond extract

Add cold water to coffee and stir until coffee is dissolved. Blend in remaining ingredients. Makes 32 punch-cup servings.

VIENNESE COFFEE

9 tablespoons instant coffee
21 cloves
3 cinnamon sticks
11 cups boiling water

¾ cup sugar
Cinnamon
Whipped cream or frozen whipped
    topping

Put cloves and cinnamon sticks in a cloth bag, and place in a saucepan with instant coffee. Pour boiling water over coffee-spice mixture. Cover and heat almost to boiling. Remove from heat and let it set, covered, for 5 minutes. Remove spice bag and stir in sugar. (If using topping, which is already sweetened, omit sugar.) Pour into cups and spoon whipped cream into each cup and sprinkle with cinnamon. Serves 15.

HOT CRANBERRY PUNCH

1 cup dark brown sugar, packed
1 cup water
½ teaspoon ground cinnamon
½ teaspoon ground cloves
¼ teaspoon ground nutmeg
¼ teaspoon ground allspice

2 16-oz. cans cranberry sauce
4 cups water
7 cups apple juice
Butter
Cinnamon Sticks

Combine sugar, 1 cup water, and spices in large kettle. Heat to boiling; then simmer. Put cranberry sauce and small amount of water in blender and liquefy. Add additional water; then add apple juice and cranberry mixture to spices. Heat to simmer. Pour into mugs; put a pat of butter on each; and garnish with cinnamon sticks. Makes about 24 mugs of punch.

ADA RUTH'S BANANA PUNCH

4 large ripe bananas
Juice of 2 lemons
2 cups frozen orange juice
3 cups pineapple juice
6 cups water

4 cups sugar
5 12-oz. cans ginger ale or lemon-
    lime drink (low-calorie ginger
    ale may be used)

Liquefy bananas in pineapple juice in blender. Combine all other ingredients except ginger ale. Freeze at least 24 hours. Take out of freezer 1 to 1½ hours before serving. Mash with potato masher and pour ginger ale over it. Serves 50.

WASSAIL

4 quarts apple juice
1 cup firmly packed dark brown sugar
1 6-oz. can frozen lemon juice concentrate
1 6-oz. can frozen orange juice concentrate

6 whole cloves
6 allspice berries
1 tablespoon ground nutmeg
24 cinnamon sticks

Combine apple juice, sugar, and undiluted juices. Tie spices in bag and drop in apple juice mixture. Cover and simmer 15-20 minutes. Remove spice bag. Serve hot in mugs, with a cinnamon stick in each. Makes 24 6-oz. servings.

SPICY MILK PUNCH

½ teaspoon ground cinnamon
½ teaspoon ground nutmeg
4 whole cloves
2½ cups orange juice

2½ cups lemon-lime soda
1 cup apple cider
1 pint vanilla ice cream

Tie cinnamon, nutmeg, and cloves in bag and soak in orange juice for one hour. Remove spices; pour in lemon-lime soda. Just before serving, divide ice cream into 10 even pieces and float it on top of punch. Makes 10 portions.

STRAWBERRY-APPLE PUNCH

2 packages frozen strawberries, thawed
1 quart apple juice

1 quart ginger ale

Mix strawberries and apple juice. Pour into punch bowl and add ginger ale. Makes approximately 15 punch cups.

PERCOLATOR PUNCH

2½ cups pineapple juice
2 cups cranberry juice
½ teaspoon allspice
½ teaspoon salt
½ cup brown sugar (lightly packed)

1¾ cups water
1 tablespoon whole cloves, broken,
        or 1 teaspoon ground cloves
3 sticks cinnamon
¼ cup lemon juice

Mix liquid in bottom of 8-cup percolator. Put dry ingredients into top of percolator. Perk for ten minutes. After perking, remove cup containing dry ingredients.

FRENCH CHOCOLATE

½ cup semi-sweet chocolate pieces
½ cup white corn syrup
¼ cup water

1 teaspoon vanilla
1 pint cream
2 quarts milk

In saucepan over low heat blend chocolate, syrup, and water until melted. Pour into bowl and refrigerate until cool. Add vanilla. Whip cream. As cream stiffens, gradually add chocolate syrup mixture. Continue beating until mixture just mounds. Spoon into bowl and refrigerate. Scald milk and pour into heated coffeepot. Spoon chocolate into cups. Pour hot milk over. Makes 16 cups.

CHRISTMAS PEPPERMINT PUNCH

2 cups lemon juice
4 6-oz. cans frozen orange juice concentrate
1 cup sugar
4 egg whites

24 hard peppermint candies
Ginger ale
24 peppermint candy canes

Mix all ingredients except candy canes and ginger ale in blender (in small amounts). Pour into punch bowl and cover with ginger ale. ·

ANOTHER PEPPERMINT PUNCH

6 quarts peppermint ice cream

12 quarts ginger ale or club soda or milk

Soften ice cream. Pour ginger ale or club soda or milk over it in punch bowl. Serves 100.

BREAKFAST IN A GLASS

1 cup milk
½ banana

Chocolate Syrup to taste
1 egg

Mix in blender and pour into tall glass.

RUSSIAN TEA

½ cup instant tea
2 cups Tang
1 package lemonade

1 teaspoon ground cloves
1 teaspoon cinnamon
2 cups sugar

Mix well and store in an airtight jar. Place 2 tablespoons of mixture in a cup of boiling water for each serving.

TEABERRY PUNCH

4 cups cold water
6 teaspoons instant, unsweetened tea
1 6-oz. can frozen concentrated lemonade

1 6-oz. can frozen concentrated limeade
1 cup cranberry juice cocktail
1 28-oz. bottle ginger ale

Mix all ingredients except ginger ale. Pour over crushed ice and add ginger ale last. Makes 20 to 25 servings.

BEST PUNCH

1 quart frozen orange juice, undiluted
¾ cup frozen lemonade, undiluted
1 can pineapple juice

2½ cups grapefruit (measure after being diluted)
1 quart water or ginger ale

Combine all ingredients. If ginger ale is to be used, add it chilled when served. Makes 1 gallon.

RAINBOW PUNCH

2 6-oz. cans frozen concentrated lemonade
1 6-oz. can frozen concentrated orange juice

1 6-oz. can frozen concentrated grape juice
1 quart ginger ale

Mix 1 can each of lemonade, orange juice, and grape juice with water as directed on the cans. Pour each juice into an ice tray or into empty juice cans. Freeze. About 15 minutes before serving, mix second can of lemonade and combine with ginger ale in a punch bowl. Add remaining cans of diluted fruit juice and fruit ice cubes.

PUNCH

6 large cans pineapple juice
2 large cans Hawaiian punch
2 large cans frozen lemonade

1 small can frozen lemon juice
4 large ginger ales
2 gallons pineapple sherbet

Mix all ingredients.

COMBINATION PUNCH

1 large can pineapple juice (46 oz.)
1 large can orange juice

1 large can apple juice
2 quarts ginger ale

Mix juices. Let stand 1 to 2 hours for flavors to blend. Pour in ginger ale before serving. Have all ingredients very cold, but may need some crushed ice. Makes 50 to 60 punch-cup servings.

CONCORD PUNCH

1 12-oz. can undiluted frozen concentrate
   Concord grape drink (or juice)
1 12-oz. can undiluted frozen concentrate pink
   lemonade

6 cups cold water
2 quarts cold orange-flavored soda
½ gallon orange sherbet

Combine grape and lemonade concentrate. Add water and stir until dissolved. Just before serving, drop scoops of sherbet on top; last, pour orange drink over all. Note: If desired, add sherbet to juice mixture. Mix with electric mixer. Add orange drink and stir. Makes 35 to 40 servings.

STRAWBERRY SMOOTHEE

6 cups cold milk
5 cups fresh strawberries
6 tablespoons sugar

6 teaspoons lemon juice
6 cups crushed ice

Place strawberries in blender. Cover with milk. Process until smooth. Mix well with other ingredients. Pour into cups and top with grated nutmeg. Makes 12 cups.

Index

Main Dishes

Beef

Company Hot Dogs, 58
Eggplant Casserole, 56
Hot Tamale Pie with Cornbread Topping, 62,63
Pepper Steak, 53
Round Steak de Parmesan, 64
Stroganoff, 58
Swiss Steak, 53
Winter Casserole, 55
Zucchini-Beef Casserole, 63

Chicken

Avis' King Ranch Chicken, 53
Chicken and Sweet Cream Biscuits, 57
Chicken Marengo, 61
Chicken Parmigiana, 62
Chicken Quiche, 58
Grapefruit Chicken Casserole, 58
Hot Chicken Salad Pinwheel, 54
Mary Alice's Chicken Enchilada Casserole, 62
Oven-Barbecued Chicken, 54
Peanut Butter Chicken, 54
Pineapple Chicken and Rice, 61
Ruby Lee's Chicken Casserole, 60
Wild Rice and Chicken Livers, 59

Eggs, Cheese

Anne's Egg Casserole, 55
Company Scrambled Eggs, 57
Connie's Creole Eggs, 65
Creamed Eggs and Ham-Danish, 60
Goldenrod Eggs, 59
Irene's Mushroom Macaroni and Cheese, 56
Linda's Eggs a la King in a Sausage Ring, 59
Mary B's Western Omelette, 59
Tex-Mex Eggs, 57

Pork

Baked Pork Chops, 56
Fruited Ham, 60
Marinated Pork Roast, 64
Pork Chops Italiano, 63
Raisin Ham, 61
Sausage Casserole, 63
Sausage and Broccoli Casserole, 65

Seafoods

Barbecued Red Snapper, 54
Cashew Tuna Casserole, 57
Hot Seafood Pie, 64
Salmon Croquettes, 60
Salmon Loaf, 60
White Fish in Cheese Sauce, 62

Veal

Veal in Cream Sauce, 55
Veal Parmesan, 61

Vegetables

Apple Yams, 72
Apricot Glazed Carrots, 80
Asparagus-Pea Casserole, 66
Bacon and Egg Stuffed Tomatoes, 81
Baked Cheese Grits, 74
Baked Spinach, 67
Beefy Baked Beans, 78
Beets and Apples, 75
Betty's Rainbow Rice, 75
Broccoli-Cheese Delight, 76
Broccoli-Potato Casserole, 69
Broccoli Sesame, 67
Carrots and White Grapes, 67
Carrot-Lima-Squash Medley, 71
Casserole Beets, 71
Cauliflower-Onion Au Gratin, 70
Chantilly Potatoes, 70
Cheese Tomato Casserole, 67
Cheesy Squash, 81
Chilled Beets and Cauliflower, 74
Corn Casserole, 67
Dilly Green Beans, 73
Easy Potato Casserole, 77
Eggplant Casserole, 79
Fried Bananas, 70
Fried Sweet Potatoes, 72
Green Beans Au Gratin, 73
Green Bean Casserole, 66
Green Beans in Sour Cream, 77
Hawaiian Baked Beans and Franks, 78
Holiday Potatoes and Peas, 75
Hot Fruit Compote, 81
Jalapeno Hot Rice, 74
Jalapeno Limas, 71
Lima Beans Creole, 79
Limas and Mushrooms, 69
Marty's Broccoli and Pea Casserole, 79
Mary Lou's Squash, 76
Mrs. Hough's Snap Beans, 75
New Potatoes with Lemon Chives, 78
Olive Potatoes, 77
Olive's Carrot and Cheese Ring, 72
Onions Almondine, 66
Onions Parmesan, 72
Orange Sweet Potatoes, 71
Parmesan Cheese Sauce, 80
Parmesan Tomatoes, 80
Peanutty Potatoes, 70
Peanutty Squash, 66
Peas in Patty Shells, 68
Potatoes Gourmet, 73
Rice-Nut Casserole, 68
Sara Ann's Potatoes, 76